Constructed Responses for Learning

Teaching students to write constructed responses does not have to become a test-prep chore. An intentional routine of constructed responses provides powerful opportunities to teach strategic thinking through writing that also deepens students' knowledge about core subjects. In this clear guide from education consultant Warren Combs, you'll learn how and why to teach students to write these short essays, no matter what subject or grade level you teach.

Special features:

- Writing prompts that are based on Webb's Depth of Knowledge (DOK) and provide practice for students at all skill levels
- Practical strategies to build critical thinking and improve students' writing, including sentence stems, acrostics, framed stories, analogies, and quad clusters
- Student self-assessment guidelines and rigorous peer-response strategies
- An interactive log to help you manage best practices and keep students engaged
- Reading-Writing Modules to help you review and implement the instructional practices and strategies
- Sample student work, at different levels, with analysis

Throughout the book, you'll find handy tools such as rubrics, logs, and checklists. These tools are also available as free eResources on our website, www.routledge.com/9781138931046, so you can download and print them for immediate use.

Warren Combs is founder of Writing to Win of Athens, Georgia, a professional development firm committed to the use of peak-performance strategies in the teaching of writing. He is also author of the bestselling *Writer's Workshop for the Common Core*.

Other Eye on Education Books Available from Routledge

(www.routledge.com/eyeoneducation)

Writer's Workshop for the Common Core:
A Step-by-Step Guide
Warren E. Combs

Empowering Students to Write and Re-Write:
Standards-Based Strategies for Middle and High School Teachers
Warren E. Combs

Focus on Text:
Tackling the Common Core Reading Standards, Grades 4–8
Amy Benjamin

Infusing Grammar into the Writer's Workshop:
A Guide for K-5 Teachers
Amy Benjamin and Barbara Golub

Teaching the Common Core Literature Standards in Grades 2–5:
Strategies, Mentor Texts, and Units of Study
Lisa Morris

Math Workshop in Action:
Strategies for Grades K-5
Nicki Newton

Close Reading in Elementary School
Diana Sisson and Betsy Sisson

Re-envisioning the Literacy Block:
A Guide to Maximizing Instruction in Grades K-8
Diana Sisson and Betsy Sisson

101 Answers for New Teachers and Their Mentors, 3rd Edition:
Effective Teaching Tips for Daily Classroom Use
Annette Breaux

Making Good Teaching Great:
Everyday Strategies for Teaching with Impact
Annette Breaux and Todd Whitaker

What Schools Don't Teach:
20 Ways to Help Students Excel in School and Life
Brad Johnson and Julie Sessions

Constructed Responses for Learning

Warren Combs

Routledge
Taylor & Francis Group

NEW YORK AND LONDON

First published 2016
by Routledge
711 Third Avenue, New York, NY 10017

and by Routledge
2 Park Square, Milton Park, Abingdon, Oxon, OX14 4RN

Routledge is an imprint of the Taylor & Francis Group, an informa business

Library of Congress Cataloging-in-Publication Data
Names: Combs, Warren E., author.
Title: Constructed responses for learning / by Warren Combs.
Description: New York, NY : Routledge, 2016. | Includes bibliographical references.
Identifiers: LCCN 2015034216 | ISBN 9781138931022 (hardback) |
    ISBN 9781138931046 (pbk.) | ISBN 9781315679983 (e-book)
Subjects: LCSH: English language—Composition and exercises—Study and teaching. |
    Composition (Language arts)—Study and teaching. | Language arts—Correlation
    with content subjects.
Classification: LCC LB1576 .C577578 2016 | DDC 372.62/3—dc23
LC record available at http://lccn.loc.gov/2015034216

ISBN: 978-1-138-93102-2 (hbk)
ISBN: 978-1-138-93104-6 (pbk)
ISBN: 978-1-315-67998-3 (ebk)

Typeset in Minion
by Apex CoVantage, LLC

Printed and bound in the United States of America by Sheridan

Contents

eResources

The book is accompanied by free bonus eResources on our website. You can access the eResources by visiting the book product page on our website: www.routledge.com/9781138931046. Click on the tab that says "eResources" and select the files. They will begin downloading to your computer.

eResources:

- Instructional Tools for Emerging and Independent Writers
- Study Session Guides for Professional Learning Teams
- Full-size templates of selected figures and tables from the book for classroom use

Meet the Author

Warren Combs, Ph.D., is founder of Writing to Win of Athens, Georgia, a professional development firm committed to the use of peak-performance strategies in the teaching of writing. A longtime researcher in the teaching of writing, he promotes classroom action research as the model for rigorous teaching and learning. He is a speaker, trainer, and author of more than nineteen titles in the teaching of writing, writing to learn content standards, and sentence-combining practice. There have been significant increases in student performance on tests of ELA, math, science, social studies, and writing in classroom action research at schools that undergo his training.

He coauthored *The Writing Process* and authored *Writer's Workshop for the Common Core* and *Empowering Students to Write and Re-Write*, in addition to several journal articles and white papers. Topics on which he regularly speaks include writing to learn the math curriculum (career, technical and agricultural education [CTAE], ELA, science, and social studies), a writing cycle for monitoring the progress of young writers, and teaching English grammar through writing. Dr. Combs has worked with administrators, teachers, and directly with students in a host of K-12 schools across the Southeast and Midwest.

His signature is demonstrating key practices in the teaching of writing with students while teachers observe from the perimeter of the room. He holds a B.A. in English, an M.A. in English linguistics, and a Ph.D. in child development and English education.

Acknowledgments

In creating a robust instructional routine of constructed responses for learning, I recognize my debt to my wife and fellow educator, Arnelle, who reviews everything I write before it goes public. My three adult children, Cortney, Erin, and Taylor, benefitted from the strategies in grades K-12 then helped me improve them to impact other students even more dramatically.

Introduction

This book presents the single, most salient truth that I have learned about teaching and learning in my career as public school teacher, university professor, researcher, and author. A well-planned, intentional system of daily short, constructed responses to core standards and related reading texts connects the dots of all other learning initiatives found in a typical K-12 curriculum. Short writing entries can become so much more than freely written responses to daily lessons and texts. They can provide much more than a source for more substantial, extended writing pieces. They can, in fact, become the centerpiece of the curriculum that ensures deep and long-lasting knowledge about core subjects designed as preparation for college and lifelong careers.

This short, practical guide implements a routine of key practices and instructional strategies that present constructed responses to standards-based lessons and reading texts. In the rush to prepare students for constructed responses in the wave of new assessments, it is critical that constructed responses not be employed as test-preparation only. There is use during the school year for constructed responses in student learning long before open-ended test items appear and long after the tests have been scored. *Constructed Responses for Learning* presents the practice of student-constructed responses to learning from the first days of school in the earliest of grades. It begins on day one as a daily and engaging tool that makes written responses as natural a classroom habit as asking to use the restroom or waiting in line at the pencil sharpener.

Section I: The Rush to Constructed Responses

Chapter 1 — Constructed Responses for Assessment and Learning (K-12 Preparation for College and Career)

The first chapter describes the rush to constructed responses that the adoption of *Common Core State Standards* has triggered with its opened-ended response test items dotting the landscape of new benchmark testing and annual assessments. A responsible way to meet this demand is a broad spectrum approach to using constructed response to support what students learn every day in every grade and subject area. Chapter 1 claims that students can be prepared for the constructed responses of test taking without interrupting solid practices of teaching and learning.

Chapter 2 – The Five Key Practices of Constructed Responses for Learning

These practices solve the teacher problem of "Whose going to grade all of this writing?" These practices pull together time-honored and well-tested instructional strategies of recent years. They include 1) quantify teacher expectations, 2) model teacher writing and student exemplars, 3) guide student choices, and a blend of two practices: 4) student self-assessment and 5) a rigorous set of PALS response strategies. These practices help trigger the natural inclination that all students can become strong, independent writers.

Chapter 3 – An Interactive Log of Constructed Responses

It takes a visible, reliable instructional tool to manage the five key practices of chapter 2 and the numerous of instructional strategies that keep students' constructed responses alive and engaged. The simplest one I've seen succeed is the Log of Entries for Teachers Expectations paired with the Log of Entries for Student Self-Check. Certainly, other tools exist or can be designed to accomplish the same goal.

Section II: Critical-Thinking Strategies That Fine-Tune Constructed Responses for Emerging and Independent Writers

Each of chapters 4 through 10 presents a critical-thinking strategy for emerging and independent writers. Pre-K through grade 1 teachers have tested and witnessed their emerging writers benefit from the strategies for emerging writers. Primary grades teachers may choose to read through only these sections in each chapter. K-12 teachers report significant benefits for their students with the strategies included for independent writers. In these chapters, writing prompts provide practice for students at all four levels of Depth of Knowledge (DOK) as indicated in this introduction.

Chapter 4 – Something on the Page That Helps You Remember What You Were Thinking (Letters, Words, Phrases, Numbers, Symbols, or Drawings)

The Remember Game prompts emerging writers through nine patterns of writing that chart their progress towards independent writing. Independent writers meet the Acrostic Vocabulary strategy that promotes learning through inductive thinking. Prompts for both of these strategies are worded to elicit responses at DOK 1—Summarizing.

Chapter 5 – Free Writing Rigorous Thought

Two strategies demonstrate how free writing responses can evidence rigor of thought. Sentence Stems for emerging writers and Focused Free Writing for independent writers combined with the five key practices can be worded to prompt responses at both DOK 1 and DOK 2—Basic Reasoning or Explaining Conceptual Knowledge.

Chapter 6 – Recalling Knowledge as Chunks in Writing

Framed Stories for emerging writers and Copy and Continue for independent writers often prompt DOK 2 responses. Both strategies make it natural for student readers to infer what texts and lessons mean instead of what they state. While the wording of the prompts in this chapter intends for student writing to show conceptual knowledge, a number of students may continue to summarize what they understand about new knowledge (DOK 1).

Chapter 7 – Sharpening Understanding of Closely Related Words (Phrases, Numbers, Symbols, or Formulas)

A single critical-thinking strategy—the Quad Cluster—benefits learning among both emerging and independent writers. Such broad-spectrum application reminds us why writing is often called the ultimate differentiator. DOK 2 is the target depth of knowledge for the Quad Cluster, yet inevitably a few students' writing will demonstrate knowledge at DOKs 1 or 3—Strategic Thinking.

Chapter 8 – Arriving in a World of Analogies (Words, Equations, Phrases, Ideas, Events, Numbers, Symbols, or Formulas)

A second critical-thinking strategy—the Analogy—differentiates learning among both emerging and independent writers. Because analogies focus more on relationship than the mean of the words, DOK 3 usually describes the depth of student thought and understanding in these responses.

Chapter 9 – From General to Specific (Telling to Showing)

Teachers' use of the Slotting strategy intends to promote strategic thought (DOK 3), yet some students' responses remain closer to the surface of understanding. Like the Framed Stories strategy, Slotting ends up serving as a productive revision strategy in extended writing.

Chapter 10 – Analyzing for Meaning

Story Reporting for emerging writers and What I Thought You Taught encourage students to move from simply reporting what a passage or lesson *said* and attempt to infer that it *meant.* Most often, this results in evidence of strategic thought (DOK 3).

Chapter 11 – Prepping for Arguments

All humans from birth have opinions. It takes practice and reactions from listeners or readers to offer a written opinion that convinces readers. In this final critical-thinking strategy—Either ... Or—students meet a trusted prompt that gives them frequent and sufficient practice with stating and supporting opinions so that their edge for presenting convincing arguments or describing a viable solution develops. Depth of knowledge evident in most Either ... Or response registers either DOK 3 or 4—Extended Thinking.

Section III: An Ultimate Learning Routine

Chapter 12 – Putting It All Together

This chapter reviews the basic practices and strategies of *Constructed Responses for Learning* with Reading-Writing Modules. All reading texts are readily available using the citations or Internet links provided. The models recognize that providing reading texts for most classroom instruction levels the playing field for all learners whether they have extensive and rich literary resources at home or not. They also show the strength of being prepared with writing prompts and teacher models geared to all levels of DOK for each text.

Chapter 13 – Launching a Parting Shot

The final chapter provides tips for placing a strong routine of constructed responses in a classroom that focuses on writing-based learning. It moves further to suggest concrete ways for teachers to organize a system of constructed responses so that all teachers have time to learn the strength and ease of implementing the strategies and practices of *Constructed Responses for Learning.*

Section I
The Rush to Constructed Responses

Chapter 1

Constructed Responses for Assessment and Learning
K-12 Preparation for College and Career

Recently, I waited on the line for a colleague to take my call, a school principal in a district that had been a long-time client of mine.

I heard, "Good morning, this is Dr. Fain.*" (*Name has been changed.) His voice carried much less of the energy I previously associated with him. I knew his district was in the final stretch of preparation for a SACS review for re-accreditation.

"Good morning to you, Doc. This is Warren Combs calling. I have a heads up for some critical training your district is offering on daily constructed responses for learning administrators. I've been asked step up the rigor in your journal routine to assure that the daily writing prompts prepare students for the coming open-response test items without sacrificing the goals of daily and weekly instruction."

"Oh, my teachers have been giving their students plenty of practice in taking the new state test items. But thanks. They have open-ended test items covered."

"I'm glad to hear it. Actually, I was referring to a sequence of journal prompts for mastering core standards at the same time they prepare students for the state tests."

"Our teachers journal three days a week like always, and they have already scheduled the month before the tests to practice constructed responses for the test."

I could tell that, in two short comments, my colleague saw constructed-response items as assessment, quite separate of instruction. I wasn't going to change this perception in this brief phone exchange. His comments echoed this narrow definition of constructed responses in the face of state tests dotted with open-ended questions; and why not? Constructed response had been so defined, and therefore underestimated, for the better part of three decades. A look at where the history of constructed responses has come since the mid-1980s explains why.

In the last years of the twentieth century, several US states sought to establish common standards among their states' curricula. The work of a handful of states made such sense that additional states signed up for inclusion in the network of states. The movement reached a tipping point, and all but three or four states adopted what has become the *Common Core State Standards (CCSS)* initiative. As the federal government infused funds into education through the *Race to the Top (RT3)* legislation (2009), it turned to the *CCSS* for guidelines for receiving those funds. Districts receiving *RT3* grants had to show evidence of standards-based learning, the workshop instructional model in every class and assessment that included open-ended questions that required written responses of students.

Constructed Responses for Assessment

Educational testing companies stepped into the action and developed new approaches to standard-based assessment. The most noticeable change became known as constructed responses to general knowledge, a provided reading text, or paired reading texts based on stated standards. A new wave of assessments for both teachers and students followed.

Constructed Responses for Assessing Teachers

The Education Testing Service (ETS) led the way in using constructed responses to assess teacher candidates for teacher certification. Its Praxis 2 test prompted these conclusions from the responses of frustrated test takers:

- Candidates expect that they cannot fully prepare writing an essay because the Praxis practice exam questions are not often well set up to score answers to a constructed response question. They expect that the hints in the questions for what is a good and bad response are easy to miss, and they are forced to rub a lucky charm as they write.
- Math majors wonder why they should be expected to write an essay when even though the ETS clearly states that a constructed response does not have to be an essay. Test takers can make charts, diagrams, or even answer in bullets.
- Many accomplished writers fail the writing portion of Praxis 2 because they misperceive it as a test on how well they write. The Praxis 2 test assesses knowledge on educational theories as listed in the Praxis 2 exam study guide and not how well test takers write. Impressive spelling, grammar, and turn of a phrase hardly matter when it comes to scoring.

ETS clarifies an important point: "Your response will be scored only on the feature listed in the scoring guide for your test." For example, explaining the rational for how you point out a difference in two points of view gets no extra points. Just stating the difference is all that is scored. What many teacher candidates don't realize is that Praxis 2 testing measures specific competencies for which they have already been prepared.

So, to succeed on the ETS Praxis 2 test with constructed-response questions takes practice. And, unfortunately, writing about what teachers who are in pre-service training are learning is not a required practice in new teacher preparation. Additionally, it's equally important to review the content of what the Praxis 2 test assesses as it is to take additional practice tests.

This point is stated in most preparation manuals that are provided for teacher candidates in state-sponsored assessments that include constructed responses. CSET (California Subject Examinations for Teachers), GACE (Georgia Assessment for the Certification of Educators), and MTEL (Massachusetts Test for Educational Licensure) are just a few of the state tests that examine teacher candidates with various degrees of constructed responses.

Constructed Responses for Assessing Students

Soon after constructed responses dotted the assessment of teacher candidates, constructed-response items for students began to appear in state assessments across the country. Maryland was one state that led the way and took great care to alleviate the anxiety of what teachers saw as a revolutionary change in teaching and learning.

A sample constructed response item for grade 3 students in Maryland looks like this.

Read this *invitation to a special party.*

You Are Invited!

What: A Grand Opening Party
Why: To celebrate the opening of

Amazing Collections!

When: Friday, July 14th
7:00 P.M. – 9:00 P.M.
Where: Rockburg Children's Museum
1905 Baker Street
Who: Come one, come all!
Cost: Free

"Amazing Collections" is a new show that will open at the Rockburg Children's Museum on Saturday, July 15th. The show will run through October 15th. Come to the grand opening party to celebrate this great new show!

Meet many young collectors and ask them about their collections. Chantz Dacus will tell you about his world-class stamp collection. Rebecca Van Meter will also be there with her collection of old and unusual buttons. You will also see collections of toy cars, stuffed animals, dolls, and even shoelaces!

There will be kids with collections of things that other people might put in the trash. Paul Johnson collects candy wrappers. Michelle Aribe has a collection of over 500 paper napkins!

"The first candy wrappers in my collection came from Brazil. I ate the candy and took the wrappers to school to show my friends. My collection just grew from there. I even have wrappers from Japan and France!"

Paul Johnson, age 8

"The first time I went to Baltimore with my parents, we ate at a restaurant with napkins that had a map of the city on them. They were great! Ever since then I have been collecting paper napkins. My favorite is one that looks like a zebra!"

Michelle Aribe, age 8

Would you like to start a collection of your own? We can help you decide what to collect and how to get started. We can even give you ideas about the best way to display your collection for everyone to see!

Bring your friends and family to a great party and help open "Amazing Collections." There will be food, fun, and prizes for everyone. It will be the world's best party!

Then answer the question below.

Explain why the museum's show is called "Amazing Collections." In your response, use information from the invitation that helps to explain your ideas. Write your answer in the box below.

Sample student response, rubric score 0 of 3

You can bring your friends and family to a great part and open Amazing collections and there will be food and prizes for everyone.

Annotation: This response is irrelevant to the question.

Sample student response, rubric score 1 of 3

The information in the invitation shows sarting a collection because thay want to teacher kids how to learn the true meaning of collecting stuff.

Annotation, using the rubric: This response demonstrates a minimal understanding of the text. The student minimally explains what the information in the invitation shows about starting a collection by stating, "thay want to teach kids how to learn the true meaning of collecting stuff."

Instructional annotation: (*While the "Annotation, using the rubric" describes the scorer's explanation for the rubric score, the "Instructional annotation" describes how the response might be improved.*) The reader answers, "thay want to teach kids how to learn the true meaning of collecting stuff." To improve this response, the reader should provide text support for wanting to teach about collecting: how kids start the process, what kids collect. . . . To further clarify the response, the reader might focus on the words "true meaning of collecting" and explain options for that idea. For example, the true meaning might simply be what is important to an individual.

Sample student response, rubric score 2 of 3

The invattation tells that the hosts of the party can help you make a collection. You might get ideas from other people so that you can may a collection of your very own.

Annotation, using the rubric: This response demonstrates a general understanding of the text. The student uses text-relevant information to explain what information in the invitation shows about starting a collection: ". . . the hosts . . . can help you make a collection. You might get ideas from other people so that you can make a collection. . . ."

Instructional annotation: The reader concludes, "the hosts of the party can help you make a collection" and then elaborates that ideas may come from other people to help you begin a collection. To improve this response, the reader could bolster support by offering specific ideas from the text like the napkin or candy wrapper collections. To extend this idea, the reader might select an item from text like shoelaces and explain why they might be significant to a collector.

Sample student response, rubric score 3 of 3

It tells you how to start a collection. Paul collected candy wrappers from countries of Japan, France and Brazil. He ate the candy first and then collected the wrappers. Michelle went to a restaurant in Baltimore to eat a restaurant. She had a napkin with a map of Baltimore on it.

Annotation, using the rubric: This response demonstrates an understanding of the complexities of the text. The student effectively uses text-relevant information to explain what information in the invitation shows about starting a collection. The student clarifies the response by giving a brief synopsis of how Paul and Michelle started their collections by paraphrasing the two stories told in the graphics of the candy wrapper and napkin.

Instructional annotation: The reader concludes that the invitation helps you know how to begin a collection and then supports and clarifies the response by summarizing the reasons for beginning two different collections in the invitation. To improve this response, the reader might further clarify that the two cited collections were started from two different impulses: the candy wrappers from attraction and the napkins from a situation.

By grade 7, Maryland students read texts for more than the recall of information in the reading text. To help teachers position the text so that students understand what response is being prompted, the state department clarifies the text for instruction.

"Scrambled Eggs"[1]

The tone of a text is the author's attitude towards his or her subject. To determine the author's tone, the reader should look at the author's word choice, grammatical arrangement of words, imagery, or vivid details, and use of metaphors.

To begin, first identify the subject. In this passage, "Scrambled Eggs," the subject is the court case against the farmer charging him $4,000 for ten scrambled eggs.

To track the clues to the author's tone, begin with the second paragraph where the farmer remembers "the few small coins" he owes the innkeeper. This detail is important; the words "few" and "small" suggest that the farmer believes that he owes only a small sum of money. However, when the farmer asks about his bill, the innkeeper gives him "a large sheet of paper covered with numbers." The discrepancy between what the farmer believes and what the innkeeper believes is central to the plot of the story and to the tracking of the author's tone. Furthermore, the detail that the amount of payment expected by the innkeeper totals $4,000 only adds to the controversy.

In paragraph four, the farmer thinks this request is "a joke." The word choice of "joke" is now the strongest indicator of the author's tone.

As the story continues, the farmer understands that he will need "a good, honest lawyer." The choice of adjectives is important because the farmer understands he will need a skilled lawyer to defend him against unscrupulous behavior. When a lawyer is found, the lawyer's reaction is outrage, another specific word choice that hearkens to the farmer's first reaction to the situation: a joke.

The next day, the lawyer is late for court and "rushed in," and he "tried to catch his breath" to respond to the judge who does not like lateness. A tiny conflict arises here, but the important element is the details about rushing and being out of breath. These details serve to set up the point of the lawyer's case. The lawyer proceeds to explain to the judge that he "was boiling two bushels of corn and planting them in my field this morning." This absurd detail connects to the farmer's initial reaction that the situation of paying $4,000 for eggs is a "joke," and further solidifies the author's tone. The lawyer's statement is met with "a roar of laughter" from people in the courtroom. The word choice "roar" speaks to the intensity of the crowd's reaction. The judge addresses the absurdity of the statement by inquiring if the lawyer has "lost your mind" and whether the lawyer believes "cooked corn will grow." The lawyer responds that "if scrambled eggs can turn into chicks" then cooked corn can grow. The images of planting cooked corn, and the transformation of scrambled eggs into chicks matches one absurdity to another.

Now the judge understands what is going on and is "outraged," which matches the lawyer's previous outrage that such a case would even go to court. The lawyer wins the case for the farmer. The lawyer is now described as "clever," which becomes an extension of the farmer's need for a "good, honest lawyer."

The author's tone or attitude about the subject of this passage could be described in a number of ways: light-hearted, bemused, comic, humorous, mirthful, playful, and so forth.

The farmer and the lawyer recognize the overall absurdity or ridiculous nature of the problem, which the lawyer makes the judge realize and which creates the tone of this passage. The author makes word choices, uses specific details, and creates certain images that allow a reader to understand selected-response test item follows:

Read the story "Scrambled Eggs" and answer the following question.

Explain what the innkeeper probably learns from his experience. In your response, use details and examples from the story that support your explanation.

The innkeeper probably learned that it's better to keep what you have. If the farmer had paid him the original cost he would have earned money. Instead he choose to charge the farmer more than what he owed. The farmer would have to pay for chickens that don't exist. Next time the innkeeper would rather settle for the 10 kroner than losing 100 kroner.

Annotation: The student states that the innkeeper learned to "keep what you have," and uses details from the story that support the suggested lesson. The student explains that had the innkeeper accepted the original amount, "he would have earned money," however, the innkeeper did not "settle for the 10 kroner," he lost 100 kroner. The additional details from the story help the student's explanation.

Read the story 'Scrambled Eggs' and answer the following question.

Explain the tone created by the author's words and phrases in paragraphs 10–12. In your response, use details and examples from the story that support your explanation. Write your answer on your answer document.

In paragraphs 10-12 the tone was humorus. The farmer's lawyer said that he was late because he was boing two bushels of corn and then planting them in his field. Then the judge asked him if he had lost his mind and the lawyer said "If scrambled eggs can turn into chicks, then why not?" The lawyer won the trial and the farmer had to pay them 50 kroner each.

Annotation: The reader identifies the tone as "humorus." What follows is a summary of the rest of the story. To improve the response the reader could use some of the text in the summary to support the humorous tone in those paragraphs. Boiling corn to plant, scrambled eggs turning into chickens, and the judge wanting to know if the lawyer had lost his mind could all serve as support for a humorous tone.

Most US states (in the *Common Core* network or not) are following the lead of states like Maryland and taking significant measures to alleviate the anxiety surrounding these new test items. It is uncertain whether these extensive explanations, student exemplars, and full-blown resources have alleviated or deepened the anxiety. Although constructed responses make up less than 20% of the weight of these new tests, schools are devoting the majority of the School Improvement or Professional Learning funds to prepare students for them. Riding on the wave of constructed responses may become one of the largest marketing efforts attracting all manner of educational publishers.

In short, most of the focus on constructed responses is on assessment. At present, publishers provide more Reading-Writing Modules that provide practice taking a test than teachers could possibly use. Unfortunately, the plethora of highly touted practice modules for test preparation are of uncertain reliability. Teachers log onto some websites in search of viable test passages for grade 4. When they take the extra step of analyzing the passage for Lexile level, they discover some are actually grade 2 and some grade 7 passages. The anxiety rises.

All of this attention on assessment overlooks a parallel use of writing to learn content standards that has progressed over the last 40 years or longer. Simple student journals or learning logs are ideas whose time have come. The remainder of this book addresses and clarifies the power of short, frequent writing to learn core standards in every course and subject of the curriculum, grades K-12.

Constructed Responses for Learning

When you turn the focus on constructed responses away from assessment and onto learning and its instructional practices, you begin to see the remarkable power in the simple processes of

1. active listening in class or close reading of texts,
2. systematic word study, and
3. constructed response (prompted or spontaneous).

From the first, it's important to note the difference between assessment and learning. First of all, by the nature of printed and digital testing, assessment with constructed responses is limited to reading texts, but classroom instruction is not and should not be. Students can construct responses to learning experiences in labs, media centers, classroom lectures, demonstrations, discussions, learning centers, oral presentations, PALS partners, small groups, video presentations, and self-guided research.

Also, constructed responses for learning can be guided by specific instructional strategies, and so they should be. When first attempting constructed responses in classroom instruction, use writing prompts to guide students' responses to new knowledge in productive ways. When students meet a broad range of the instructional strategies systematically, they begin to discern which is best to use in analyzing, explaining, reflecting on, or responding to what they have been taught or what they have read.

Additionally, constructed responses for learning include oral as well as written presentations. It's important to note that oral responses are most efficiently taught through writing. When students experience extensive practice in writing, their confidence in oral responses sharpens implicitly. You will notice increased confidence and competence among your students in class discussions, oral reports, small group planning, and questions they ask about what you are teaching.

Lastly, instruction with embedded constructed responses can focus on student learning as much as teacher instruction. Students can be working as hard at acquiring a variety of critical-thinking strategies as we teachers do at presenting them systematically. Whatever strategies we prompt students to acquire, the overall routine needs to include as much direction for students as it does for teachers. To this end, five key practices have emerged to ensure that students are as engaged in their learning as their teachers are. Continue to prompt each of these practices directly until students show clear evidence that they select a strategy, write an entry, self-assess, and respond to a PALS entry[2] without prompting.

	Key Practice	Rationale
1	Quantify your expectations for each constructed response.	If you do not tell students upfront how much they need to write or how many specific features need to be in their writing, many of them ask, "How long does it have to be?" or "Do we have to use words from the word wall?" So save time and simply quantify the number of sentences and key terms you expect. **Note:** The number of key terms students used meaningfully trumps the number of sentences. If students use and/or explain more of the key terms than you expect in fewer sentences than you expect, their performance exceeds expectations.
2	Model the strategy underlying the constructed response that you prompt students to write.	The first time you introduce a strategy for a constructed response, read aloud and/or show students a model of the response you constructed on the topic you gave them. That is the sure way to show them the connection among the topic, the prompt, and the strategy. Yes, some of them will attempt to imitate precisely what you wrote. Yet if they do, they practiced following the strategy you want them to acquire. On subsequent prompts with the same strategy, simply write along with your students. Writing with students shows that you value what you are asking them to do.
3	Guide student choices with a simple critical-thinking strategy.	Critical-thinking strategies that prompt student writing abound. In this book, you'll find a dozen that fit these criteria: 1) short (10–15 minutes to write 4–7 sentences and record a PALS response), 2) consistently prompts critical thought, and 3) becomes a mental construct for students to use as they respond to constructed-response items on state and national tests.
4	Prompt specific PALS strategies with each entry.	For several decades, educational leaders have championed peer-responses at the close of a daily workshop session. Unfortunately, the resulting strategies are too often presented:

	Key Practice	Rationale
		• Generically: for all manner of writing, student writers ask a partner or small group, "Tell me what part of the writing you like best" or "What do you want to know more about?" • In a fashion best defined as "loosey-goosey": teachers expect students to think about their writing before they join a partner and share what they have written and listen to how their partner chooses to react spontaneously. Neither of these fit within the 10–15 minutes for students to write an entry of critical thought and elicit a rigorous response from assigned PALs. Nor do they document any details of the transaction between writer and a PAL.
5	Secure student self-assessment.	Research and practice from the 1990s established student self-assessment as essential to peak-performance learning among all groups of students. Jan Chappuis and colleagues identify this process of teacher-coached, student self-assessment as an example of formative assessment.[3] As students assess their own performance, they acquire (form) the awareness of what makes writing strong. Like PALS response strategies, self-assessment routines and rubrics must be concrete, specific, and easy for students to understand and use.

Of the five practices, the first two emphasize the role you play in setting the practices in motion. At first, you set expectations high enough to stretch students' minds, yet not so high to discourage their spirits. Then you model what you expect in your own writing. Truth be known, until you write exactly what you expect students to write, you can't be sure that what you expect can be written in the 10 to 15 minutes allowed for writing and sharing.

The last three practices, then, shift to an emphasis on the roles that students play in keeping the momentum of the writing task alive. First they write, keeping in mind the guide of the critical-thinking strategy that you positioned. Then they self-assess their writing, declaring whether their entries exceed, meet, or approach your expectations on three writing probes. A PAL joins them to let them show evidence of the assessment of each probe in their writing and record what their PALs say is strong about quality of their writing.

Two more points remain in planning an effective scope and sequence of writing tasks that uses the full power of constructed responses. First of all, the precise nature of the writing is essential to keep in mind. Constructed responses for learning (and assessment, for that matter), focus on specific content learning, not on the elaboration of how it was learned. Writers of constructed responses do not receive credit for writing especially well, unless they include the details and vocabulary of specific content prompted. Constructed responses for learning include

- A response to new knowledge that is
  - Taught (based on a core standard)
  - Read (a passage of appropriate Lexile provided)
- One draft (with freedom to return and improve the content of written responses on the students own time)
  - A specific number of key terms (equations, formulas, icons, numbers, phrases, or symbols)
  - Short (3–10 sentences)
  - Frequent (average of 3 entries per week)
  - Unedited for language conventions
  - Un-scored for language conventions
  - Written and shared orally with a designated PAL in 10 to 15 minutes
  - Certain to prompt critical thought

Finally, the scope and sequence of constructed responses is critical. There are a myriad of critical-thinking strategies that have become available to teachers over the last 40 years. All of them have merit, but only a few fit into the five practices of effective learning above that make sure the writing supports the lesson of the day without consuming much of the time allowed for the lesson itself. This book identifies 22 strategies. Together, the writing prompts, the practices, and the strategies form a structured system for building students' habits for analysis, explanation, and response they can use throughout their school years.

Additionally, the scope and sequence of writing prompts moves students through a progress of increased comprehension. Even though there is a growing selection of models for levels of comprehension available, a quick review shows their similarities.

	Source	Levels of Comprehension
1	Bloom's *Taxonomy of Educational Objectives* (1956)	Translation, interpretation, extrapolation
2	Marzano, *Dimension of Thinking* (1988)	Gathering, organizing, analyzing, generating, integrating, evaluating information
3	*Reading Excellence Act* (REA, 1998)	Two levels of processing: shallow (low-level understanding) and deep (high-level application)
4	*Reading First* Initiative (2002)	Two levels of processing: shallow (low-level understanding) and deep (high-level application)
5	*Depth of Knowledge* (1997)	Recall, basic reasoning [skill/concept], strategic thinking, extended thinking
6	Fisher and Frey, *TDQ: Text-Dependent Questions* (2015)	What the text says, how it works, what it means, what it inspires you to do

The six sources include from 3 to 6 levels of thinking or comprehension that move through tasks that are 1) literal, 2) inferential, 3) evaluative, and 4) appreciative.

Each source has had widespread impact and is well-described elsewhere, yet the model for this book is *Depth of Knowledge*. It's a practical choice for two reasons:

- This model for aligning standards with curriculum is widely accepted among US states and familiar to many classroom teachers.
- Level 4 of *DOK* requires investigation and time to think, so it provides an opportunity to show how constructed responses can, and do, readily move beyond on-demand writing into productive extended writing and thinking.

Therefore, the 12 critical-thinking strategies described in the following pages appear as examples of how they prompt and track students' comprehension of new knowledge at the levels of 1) recall, 2) basic reasoning (skill/concept), 3) strategic thinking, and 4) extended thinking. They all fit within the Five Key Practices with ease, and classroom action research has confirmed that their impact on comprehension of new knowledge is significant and long lasting. A report of the results of systematic use of these strategies on independent tests of student performance appears at www.writingtowin.com/research-based-routines/results/.

Notes

1. http://internet.savannah.chatham.k12.ga.us/schools/hms/staff/Alley/Shared%20 Documents/Scrambled%20Eggs.pdf
2. PALS (Peer-Assisted Learning System) refers to a set of specific, intentional response strategies designed to guide students in their responses to each other's writing. For example, in response to a constructed response written in the informative/explanatory genre, a PALS strategy provides three choices to use: "What stands out in your writing is the 1) clear main idea, 2) supporting details, or 3) related example." PALs pick the one that best fits the writing, and the writers record it in the margin of their writing.
3. Jan Chappuis, Rick J. Stiggins, Steve Chappuis, Judith A. Arter, eds. *Classroom Assessment for Student Learning: Doing It Right - Using It Well.* 2nd edition, 2006.

Chapter 2

The Five Key Practices of Constructed Responses for Learning

The expectation that every student in the school will be successful in college—emphasis on *every*—makes students and the adults in their lives move mountains. I have come to believe that the so called "soft bigotry of low expectations" is the most fundamental of our challenges in education.[1]

I introduce a critical-thinking strategy to seventh grade students new to writing constructed responses for learning. I call the strategy the Quad Cluster; it's the strongest vocabulary builder I've found for writing on demand (see chapter 7). To the eight teachers observing from the back of the classroom as the video camera recorded, I said, "Watch these students start thinking critically about their current course standard in the next two minutes." The comment caught their attention just as I hoped. After all, nothing important can possible happen that quickly, right? They were prepared for a surprise.

"I see that you have 12 math terms on the word wall. As we write today, we all need to use 4–5 of those key terms in our writing. Write *4–5 key terms* at the top of page 9 of your journals."

"Next, turn to the front of your journals and read aloud with me what we are to do for Strategy E, the Quad Cluster."

All the students and teachers found the page titled "Guide for Writing to Learn."

"We'll read this like a choir sings, but please no singing. Simply read each of the four guides aloud together, beginning with guide #1 that starts with the word *list*. All together now."

Everyone in the room reads aloud in unison, "List the four terms at the top of your journal page."

"Turn to page 9 and list the four words on the top line."

Students and teachers wrote divisor, quotient, difference, product. I expected them to and they did. We continued by reading guide 2 aloud together and did as the guide directed, "Circle the word that is different from the other three." For those that were hesitant to choose, I prompted, "Go ahead and circle *divisor*." I knew it was the choice that left three words that were alike. After all, constructed responses for learning isn't about choosing the logical answer but explaining why it is logical.

After we read guides 3 and 4 in succession—"Write 2–3 sentences explaining why the circled word is different" and "Write 2–3 more words explaining why the other three are alike"—a student blurted out, "You mean we have to write 4–6 sentences about these four words?"

"Let's see," I appeared to be puzzled, held page 8 of my journal up close to my eyes and feigned reading the guidelines over again, this time quite analytically. "Hm, 2–3 + 2–3? What's that? Yes, I believe that's it: 4–6 sentence + 2 or more additional key terms from the word wall."

I returned my gaze to the inquirer, relieved. "Yes, that's what it says. I guess you and I had better get busy" and sat down to write in my journal. When my bottom hit the seat of the chair, I continued my expectations, "We all have five minutes to write. Get your pencils moving."

Since I knew students' biggest problem in writing on demand is getting started, I suggested, "Begin with the sentence, 'Divisor is the different word in this cluster.' There, I've given you your first sentence. You can thank me now or thank me later." Several students chuckled; some said, "thanks"; and they all got busy writing.

Those seventh graders had never been asked to write an explanation of a math topic in their own words before, yet they all wrote four or more sentences. Eight of them wrote seven sentences or more. The students were proud, and in a debriefing session, their teachers voiced surprise: "I can't believe what I just saw; I have some of those students in science, and they haven't written more than one decent sentence in five minutes all year. You've got some kind of magic over them."

Actually, no magic at all. It's plain and simple expectations, expectations that are specific, intentional, doable, and yet positioned so that students have to stretch beyond what they have been asked to do before. Simply begin by quantifying your expectations for constructed responses:

- Number of key terms (phrases, symbols, or even formulas) used with meaning
- Number of meaningful sentences
- Cited evidence from one, two, or three parts of the lesson/text
- A connection of their own writing (text) to their experience (self), the lesson (text), or general knowledge (world).

One of the teachers in the debriefing session, "This routine all makes good sense. My kids always ask, 'How long does it have to be?' This way I tell them before they get a chance to ask. Saves time."

"Exactly, and sets the minds and pens of students running," I replied, "Start with expectations of the number of key terms and sentences for the first few times you prompt students to write on demand. Then add citing evidence and text connections later."

Let's see what some of the students wrote that day:

Exceeded expectations (10 key terms with meaning, 7 meaningful sentences)

Divisor is the different term in this cluster. It is part of the problem in a division. Division is a math operation with a divisor, dividend and quotient. Difference, quotient and product are the results of math operations. Difference is the result of subtraction. Product is the result of multiplication, and quotient is the result of division. They are from all of the operations except addition.

Met expectations (6 key terms with meaning, 5 meaningful sentences)

Divisor is the different term in this cluster. It is not an answer like quotient, difference and product. It is part of a problem, and quotient is the answer. Difference is the answer to a subtraction problem. Product is the answer in multiplication.

Approached expectations (3 key terms with meaning, 3 meaningful sentences; sentences 2 through 4 express an opinion about the difficulty of the task.)

Divisor is the really strange here. It is complicated and hard to explain. How to put one number into another is very hard to say in words. Try it and you will see what I mean in a heartbeat. The other three words are all easy. They are all answers to math operations except for addition.

Expectations for Emerging Writers

Fortunately, for emerging writers, the Quad Cluster strategy is itself concrete and similar to how they think. From early infancy children play with buttons, balls, or blocks and group them according to their differences. Picking a science term that is the different one among four is not an unfamiliar task. With students who are not independent writers, they do the thinking, and their teacher does the writing. In a kindergarten class, I wrote the four-word prompt on chart paper:

dog, cat, goldfish, gerbil

The group of six students seated around the flipchart watched me write. I said, "One of these words is not like the other. One of these words is different.

Can anyone tell me which one?" Without hesitating, one eager student raised his hand and declared, "*Goldfish* is different! It's a fish but not the others."

"Wow," I responded, "You guys are quick. Let me write this down: 'Goldfish is the different word. It is a fish but not the others.'"

"Now we are **not** finished just yet," I cautioned them, "Someone needs to tell me what to write about how the other three words are alike. Use some of the words from the science word wall." They all took a quick look at the words on the wall.

"Oh, I know. *A dog is a **animal**,*" pipes up one of the girls.

I reply, "That is true, but is that how a dog is different from a goldfish?"

"No," said two others. "A goldfish is a animal, too." They all agreed, and it became silent for 15 to 20 seconds as the students return their gaze to the word wall (an eternity in kindergarten).

I decide to think hard as well, then spoke, "Hm, how about this, let's look at the word wall and find a word that goes with *dog, cat,* and *gerbil,* but not with goldfish." The students moved their gaze around the words for some time until one small voice queried, "Mammal?" The rest thought it was a good choice, and one student served up a sentence without being asked.

"A dog is a mammal." So I wrote it after the first two sentences in paragraph form.

"And so is a cat and a gerbil," said another student without hesitation.

I led the students in reading all four sentences aloud and asked, "Who'd like to wrap this writing up with a final sentence?"

After a good bit of thinking, one spoke up, "And that's why they are not a fish."

"No, No," another said. "That's not right. It's not *because*. They are just mammals and the goldfish is a fish." I quickly wrote, "They are just mammals and the goldfish is a fish." We read the five sentences aloud together as I pointed to the sentences, and satisfied, the six students and I disbanded to another activity.

As I walked out to a debriefing room with the observing teachers, I saw the kindergarten teacher tear off the constructed response from the flipchart and post it next to three constructed response stories written by other groups of six students earlier that week. I knew that he would coach students in "reading" their own group writing and eventually that of other student groups throughout the week until the next constructed response was posted.

Quantified expectations? Oh yes, indeed.

- One or more sentences about why *goldfish* is different
- One or more sentences about why the other three words are alike
- A sentence that wraps up the thought
- Two or more key words used from the current word wall to write about the four words in the Quad

Note that I did not expect students to explain fully how mammals and fish differed. I did, however, expect them to state that they were different and label this with a key word from the word wall. In this case, the difference was the classification of animals, three mammals and a fish.

The demonstration shows how kindergarten students readily move beyond the recall of DOK 1 responses to DOK 2. I met the core writing standard for the informative/explanatory genre by modeling how to compare and contrast. Further, it engaged students' minds to parlay an inherent tendency to compare and contrast groups of objects to comparing and contrasting words.

Expectations for College-Bound Writers

Staying with the Quad Cluster strategy, I worked with Advanced Placement US history students as they studied the decades leading up to the US Civil War. Their teacher helped me project a Quad Cluster on the interactive board for them to jot down on the next page of the journal section of their history notebooks.

state's rights, slavery, territorial expansion, US Civil War*

This time, the different term was marked with an asterisk (*). The students knew what to do. Let's see what they knew. Here's Carlene's entry, a student who exceeded my expectations.

> The US civil war is the different term in this cluster since it is the result of the other three terms, state's rights, slavery and territorial expansion. It is better to say state's rights, slavery and territorial expansion were <u>factors</u> that led to the US civil war. There are different opinions about which factor was stronger, but in five minutes, I treat them as even. State's right separated the north from the south; was a <u>doctrine</u> of southern states that mistrusted a <u>strong federal government</u>. Northern states understood how important the <u>Federal Bank</u> and the <u>federal court system</u> were in their daily lives. Slavery was another division; white people who owned black people were <u>sanctioned</u> in the south and not in the north. With the <u>Kansas-Nebraska Act of 1854</u>, territorial expansion became tense. The south insisted that half of the new territories become slave states regardless of what the people in the territories believed, and the civil war was bound to happen.

Later, I received an email from Carlene's teacher and an attachment of Carlene's extended entry. Every three weeks, students selected one constructed response to expand into an extended writing piece. You can see that Carlene used further investigation to extend her writing (and her thinking).

> The US civil war was caused by several factors. The doctrine of state's rights, differences in laws about slavery and territorial expansion all played

an important part. There are different opinions about which factor was strongest. I've always lived in the south, and I was taught that state's right was the major cause of the "War between the States." As I grew older and read more, I realized that territorial expansion and slavery were even stronger factors. All sources I have read this week show how slavery was the major cause of the US civil war.

Today many white southerners today totally disagree and won't change their minds. They mistrust any law that supports the <u>federal government</u>. In the "Top Five Causes of the Civil War," Martin Kelly states that southern states fought against the US Constitution from the beginning. John C. Calhoun of South Carolina sponsored a bill that would allow states to nullify federal laws they didn't like. That sounds strange today for sure. It didn't in the south. When nullification was defeated, and "the southern states felt they were no longer respected, they moved towards secession." By contrast, northern states understood how important the <u>Federal Bank</u> and the <u>federal court system</u> were in their daily lives. While states' right was an active issue prior to the civil war, it was not the greatest influence. That recognition goes to slavery; it was the main reason southern state fought for states' rights.

Slavery caused enormous division; white people owning black people was <u>sanctioned</u> in the south, but not in the north. Life as southerners knew it could not survive if <u>abolition</u> succeeded. So as the country expanded to the west, our textbook posed "a question of whether new states admitted to the union would be <u>slave or free</u>." Henry Clay's Compromise of 1850 tried to keep the balance between slave and free states with <u>popular sovereignty</u>, but it did just the opposite. The tension exploded when Kansas voted to be a free state. Mr. Kelly noted that "the fight even erupted on the floor of the senate when anti-slavery proponent Charles Sumner was beat over the head by South Carolina's Senator Preston Brooks." Without the hope of slavery, the south felt doomed, and the only choice was to secede. Southern states stayed around while the federal government reduced states' right to have a separate bank and justice system. When it came to slavery, they acted immediately. <u>Abraham Lincoln</u> was elected President when he campaigned to end slavery everywhere and won. After he was elected, seven states succeeded before Lincoln was sworn in to office two months later.

This shows me that the civil war was mostly about slavery. Southerners said states' rights caused secession; their actions showed the real cause.

— Carlene[2]

Note the expectations that Carlene's writing exceeded. Her teacher expected that his students' extended writing pieces

- use 8 to 10 key terms (words, phrases, symbols, formulas) from their lessons and reading texts;
- produce an extended argument that included a claim in a beginning section, a conclusive ending paragraph, and a multi-paragraph body of reasons; and
- cite two pieces of evidence from class lessons and one outside source.

Setting specific, intentional expectations ensures that students master what I've learned to call the Five Key Practices of writing-based learning. Quantify Teacher Expectations is Key Practice #1. The others are

- Model Teacher Writing,
- Guide Student Choices, and
- Prompt PALS Responses, through
- Secured Student Self-Assessment.

These four key practices are all ignited by rigorous expectations that help you

- write a model constructed response that exceeds your own expectations,
- choose the critical-thinking strategy promotes optimal understanding,
- select a PALS strategy that focuses students talk on the quality of writing, and
- tie self-assessment directly back to your stated expectations.

Let's summarize the Five Key Practices that you will see applied extensively throughout the remaining chapters. A mnemonic that helps me keep them in my mind each time I prompt students to write is QM-GPS. It's my Quiet Motion Global Positioning System. Unlike the GPS in my automobile, it doesn't talk to me, tell me I made a wrong turn and with resignation, announce that it was re-calculating my trip once again. Instead, as I keep the Five Key Practices in focus, I benefit from seeing students understand my writing prompt with ease. The students benefit from producing optimal thoughts to share with PALs for responses of substance.

Quantify Teacher Expectations

Before students ask, "How much do we have to write," project the number of

- key terms from a word wall, lesson, or reading text;
- sentences;
- citations to part of a lesson/text; and
- connections to self, text, or world,

depending on the ability and experiences of your students.

Model Teacher Writing

Ideally, the first time you prompt students to write a constructed response with a critical-thinking strategy, write your model entry ahead of time so you can read it aloud for your students' benefit. Writing the entry in advance also lets you test if the entry can be written in 5 to 7 minutes with benefit. As students begin to write, be sure to sit and write along with them for the first minute or two before you move about to coach those whom you see need the support.

Every time I prompt students to write, I write with them. Since I'm a visitor to classrooms, there is rarely time to prepare a model in advance. Thankfully, research from the 1980s established the positive impact of teachers' writing along as their students write.

Guide Student Choices

Simply select a critical-thinking strategy from the "Guide for Writing to Learn" (see eResources) and introduce the strategy quickly and efficiently.

- Read your written model of the entry you have prompted for students to write.
- Lead the students in reading each guideline in the strategy aloud, together. Allow enough time for students to apply each guideline before reading the next one aloud, together.
- Briefly remind students of the expectations you have quantified.

You likely know of other critical-thinking strategies for prompting writing in addition to the *W2W* strategies. 3–2–1, the Frayer model, K-W-L, and any of eight thinking maps are just a few. Insert all strategies into the Five Key Practices. They assure that all critical-thinking strategies are used to their fullest advantage.

Prompt PALS Responses and Student Self-Assessment

Select a PALS response strategy (pp. 162–163) that best accompanies the writing that you have completed with your students. PALS responses combine with student self-assessments to provide immediate and beneficial feedback using rubrics for all K-12 students. The first rubric supports the self-assessment and PALS response of emerging writers, many kindergarten students, and a decreasing number of students in grades 1 and 2. Note that this rubric allows only one PALS response option. From my experience, emerging writers can count their number of key words and sentences/facts. They compare the numbers of each in their writing and circle: whether they had more, fewer, or exactly the number

KEYWORDS	SENTENCES	PALS RESPONSE

exceed   meet   approach   exceed   meet   approach   voice   picture   flow

you expected. As PALs, they soon learn to identify a strong voice, pictures, or flow in the writing that they hear read aloud.

The rubric for independent, K-2 writers includes the same two statements for self-assessment, but the options for PALs expands. PALs are expected to listen to their assigned writers read their writing aloud and explain their two self-assessment scores. PALs then circle either a check (√) or question mark (?) to agree or question the explanation for each score. They then proceed to identify what stands out most among three features of writing quality in the writing:

- Voice, pictures, or flow for all writing
- Main idea, supporting details, or both for informative/explanatory writing
- Opinion, reasons, or details for opinion pieces
- An additional response task that they write under "Other" to use

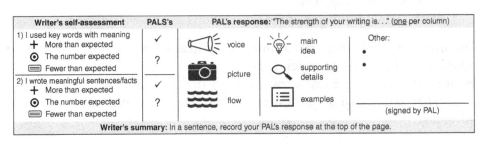

The rubric for all other independent writers includes a third statement for self-assessment that prompts students to identify the number of times they cite evidence from a text or lesson. Once PALs listen to the assigned writers' explanation of the three self-assessment scores, they circle either a check (√) or question mark (?) for each of the three. PALs conclude by identifying what stands out in 2 to 4 features of writing quality in student writing.

- Voice, pictures, or flow for all writing
- Main idea, supporting details, or both for the informative/explanatory genre
- Claims, reasons, or alternate claims for the argumentative genre
- Any additional response task that they write in under "Other" to use

Writer's self-assessment <u>first</u>, then PAL's check					
1) I used key words with meaning	**PAL's**	2) I wrote meaningful sentences/facts	**PAL's**	3) My writing shows evidence from	**PAL's**
+ More than expected ◉ The number expected ▱ Fewer than expected	✓ ?	+ More than expected ◉ The number expected ▱ Fewer than expected	✓ ?	+ 3+ parts of the text ◉ 2 parts of the text ▱ 1 part of the text	✓ ?

PAL's response: "The strength of your writing is. . ." (circle <u>one</u> per assigned column)

Your writing	Information genre	Argument genre	Other	
• voice	• main idea	• claim	•	
• pictures	• related details	• reasons	•	
• flow	• examples	• alternate claim	•	(signed by PAL)

Writer's summary: In a sentence, record your PAL's response at the top of the page.

Remarkably, students from all demographics find the interactive rubrics engaging, and the large majority of them complete them with precision. Fortunately for you, the weight of scoring and writing comments on all student writing is removed from your shoulders. Instead of "grading" writing, you simply check students' precision in using the interactive rubrics and conference with small groups of those who need coaching.

After a few weeks of writing constructed responses to learn course standards in the context of the Five Key Practices, students eagerly complete their writing to find out the response of a PAL assigned to them for 2 to 3 weeks.

- Students review their constructed responses and complete three self-assessment statements:
  - I used key terms with meaning; the writer circles (+) for exceeding, (◉) for meeting, or (=) for approaching.
  - I wrote meaningful sentences.
  - I cited evidence from 1, 2, or 3 parts of the lesson/text.
- Students read their entries aloud to their PALs and show evidence in their writing for each of their self-assessments.
- Their PALs check the student writers' explanation for each statement with ✓ for agreeing with the explanations and ? for questioning them.
- Next PALs record their PALS response by completing the sentence stem: "The strength of your writing is. . . .," circling a response on 2 to 3 three-part PALS response strategies designated by their teachers.
- Student writers summarize their PALs' responses in their own words at the top of the page.

A very promising alternative to interactive scoring with printed rubrics, pencils, and paper is online self-assessment, PALS check, and response. In 2015–2016, over 2,500 grade 3–10 students are piloting *W2Win* UNDERSTANDINGS online. A screenshot shows you how helpful a neutral instructional tool like an LMS (learner management system) is when the LMS makes certain that

- writers perform the self-assessment immediately when they save their writing;
- designated PALs sign in to check the writer's self-assessment after the writers read their entries aloud;

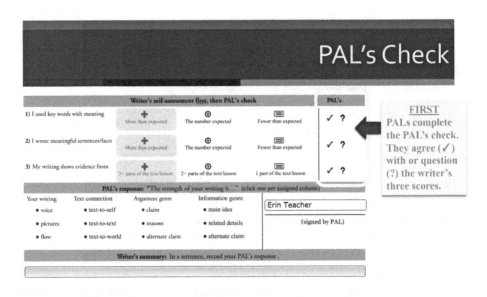

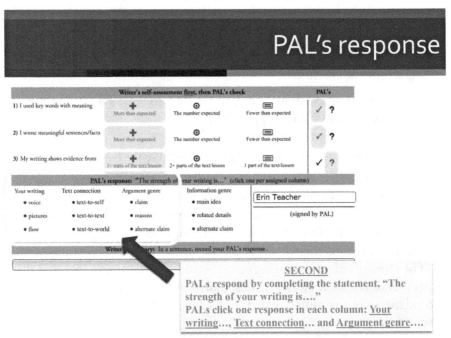

- PALs responds on a three-part PALS response strategy to all;
- writers summarize their PALs' responses with a sentence in the field provided; and,
- once this interaction is complete, the writers submit their writing to their teachers online.

Using these Five Key Practices, each time you prompt students to write has several notable benefits. They help writing constructed responses for learning

- Fit seamlessly within standard-based lessons, not feel like something extra tacked onto an already full lesson.
- Keep you from having to respond to every entry your students write. Our students need to be writing much more than we teachers have time to read.
- Empower students to self-assessment of writing in ways you can trust.
- Coach students to respond to the quality of each other's writing with substance and benefit.
- Ensure peak-performance of students on tests of grade-level knowledge and written expression (constructed and extended responses).

Brain-Focused Vocabulary

While the Five Key Practices amount to the centerpiece of this book, one critical point remains. It's the words we use when we talk to students about writing. For generations we have used terms like

Style, referring to the personality of the writer in the writing
Ideas, referring to writing content
Organization, referring to the arrangement

Unfortunately,

Style as dress or personal behavior in groups overpowers students' understanding of *style* in writing.
Ideas as intelligence pervade students' understanding of content and meaning in writing.
Organization is little understood by students who show little evidence of organization in their personal lives.

Constructed Responses for Learning uses three terms attributed to Flannery O'Connor in her career as trainer of English teachers. Her English-teacher students recall her reminder: *voice, pictures,* and *flow*; that's all they need to know.

Use your **voice** . . . to show atmosphere, **attitude, confidence,** conviction, disposition, **energy, emotion, feeling,** frame of mind, **happiness, humor,** individuality, manner, **mood,** nature, novelty, passion, **personality,** pitch, point of view, precision, **sadness,** sensation, **temper** (good or bad), **tone** or uniqueness

Make **pictures** with your words . . . to bare, bring to light, clarify, **demonstrate, describe,** depict, detail, disclose, **display,** establish, exemplify, exhibit, **explain,** explicate, expose, flesh out, **give details, illustrate, make clear,** portray, prove, represent, reveal, **show,** show evidence of, stage, substantiate, tell all or **uncover**

Let your thoughts **flow** . . . to **arrange, assemble,** associate, attach, blend in, catalog, categorize, classify, combine, connect, coordinate, correlate, gift-wrap, group, join, link, link up, package, position, **put in order,**

put together, record, relate, shape, sort, sort out, **sequence, smooth out,** systematize, tie or transition.

(**Bold-faced** words have worked well with elementary students.)

While few students believe they have impressive style, important ideas or a knack for organization, they all know that they

- have voices;
- can identify, visualize, and describe pictures;
- recognize when language flows (makes sense) and when it doesn't.

In every class that I visit to coach students in the art of constructed response, I leave a wall chart or PDF of this chart. It reminds them that all writing has *voice, pictures,* and *flow,* and their best writing has just the right balance of the three to reach the minds of their readers with their thoughts.

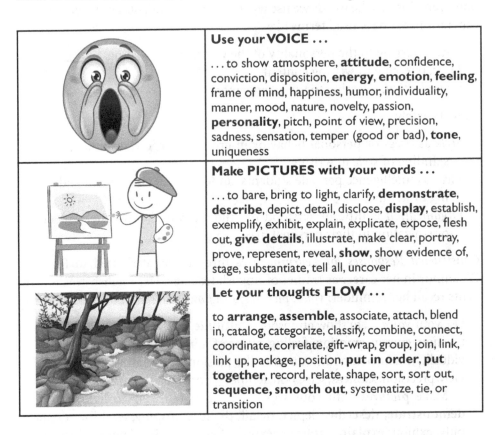

	Use your VOICE . . .
	. . . to show atmosphere, **attitude**, confidence, conviction, disposition, **energy, emotion, feeling,** frame of mind, happiness, humor, individuality, manner, mood, nature, novelty, passion, **personality**, pitch, point of view, precision, sadness, sensation, temper (good or bad), **tone,** uniqueness
	Make PICTURES with your words . . .
	. . . to bare, bring to light, clarify, **demonstrate, describe**, depict, detail, disclose, **display**, establish, exemplify, exhibit, explain, explicate, expose, flesh out, **give details**, illustrate, make clear, portray, prove, represent, reveal, **show**, show evidence of, stage, substantiate, tell all, uncover
	Let your thoughts FLOW . . .
	to **arrange, assemble**, associate, attach, blend in, catalog, categorize, classify, combine, connect, coordinate, correlate, gift-wrap, group, join, link, link up, package, position, **put in order, put together**, record, relate, shape, sort, sort out, **sequence, smooth out**, systematize, tie, or transition

Summing Up

Constructed responses for learning follow a different routine than the constructed responses we and our students meet in the new wave of state and national assessment. Since constructed responses for learning provides a scaffold of the Five Key Practices described in this chapter, they

- produce writing that is longer and more substantial than open-ended test items,
- translate into increased student use of key terms of course standards in classroom discussions,
- accelerate the retention of new knowledge exponentially,
- differentiate learning to students with varied learning styles and ability levels,
- Close the achievement gaps among student subgroups in a school year.[3]

In other words, when you include the Five Key Practices each time you prompt students to write, they explain most fully what they know in writing. Additionally, the power of the Key Practices is increased when you use student-friendly terms to refer to the traits of writing like *voice, pictures*, and *flow*. When you use these three words, you find it easier to talk about writing, and you see how much more readily your students talk about the *voice, pictures*, and *flow* in their writing. More than any other three words, these three help students feel that it is natural and normal for them to learn and to express what they have learned as confident, independent writers.

Looking Ahead

The next chapter turns to classroom environment. It offers a viable answer to a critical question "What are the instructional tools and procedures in classroom instruction that make the best use of the Five Key Practices of writing-based learning?"

Notes

1. Harold Brown, The Importance of High Expectations, October 17, 2012, www.edworkspartners.org
2. http://americanhistory.about.com/od/civilwarmenu/a/cause_civil_war.htm
3. www.writingtowin.com/research-based-routines/results/

Chapter 3

An Interactive Log of Constructed Responses

Having the physical environment of the classroom well arranged is one of the ways to improve the environment of learning and to prevent occurrence of problematic behaviors. Research on the environment of a classroom has shown that the physical arrangement can affect the behavior of students as well as teachers. A well structured classroom tends to improve the academics and the behavioral outcomes of students.[1]

It's a Bird! ... It's a Plane! ... It's Superman!

These familiar words charged my curiosity as I hurried home to watch Superman reruns after school in the afternoons early in my school years. Today, the three phrases remind me of the varied reactions from teachers when I show them a student exemplar of an interactive learning log of constructed responses. I simply say what I know to be true, "Learning logs like this one are the key to optimal learning every day in every class." The responses essentially say, "I know what you're talking about," that is, before they see the routine for constructed responses in action.

- I've tried journals. Most of the writing soon becomes repetitious self-talk: **It's a diary!**
- Journals just show that student vaguely understand what I teach: **It's a journal!**
- This learning log looks like what my students write. Since they started writing daily in their journals explaining key terms like these, their use of the language of math has grown amazingly. My kids can talk math like no group I've taught before: **It's an interactive log of constructed responses!**

I would be remiss if I claimed that the interactive log is a magical stand-alone because it certainly is not. You've already met the Five Key Practices of chapter 2 that contribute significantly to optimal learning and writing. To these practices, it is important to add characteristics of a classroom conducive to optimal learning. Lists of characteristics dot the Internet, one of the most concise sources is teachthought (www.teachthought.com). The website reviews how technology, social media, and software applications relate to improved classroom instruction. The ideas there may foreshadow the way teachers teach and students learn within the next few decades. To be sure, the website's approach to learning environment is in line with the best ideas educators have discovered over the last 30 years. Some of the stated characteristics for a highly effective learning environment include the following.

Classroom Environment That Support Constructed Reponses for Learning

Questions are valued over answers. No doubt. That's why all the writing strategies in these pages prompt students to think critically, often divergently. When students recall ideas from a source, they reconfigure the ideas, not simply regurgitate them. In addition, students are given the *answers* in strategies E (Quad Cluster) and L (Analogy) so they spend no time searching for a logical or accurate answer. Instead, they are rewarded for explaining and inquiring why a provided choice is logical.

Ideas come from divergent sources. The techniques and strategies in these chapters come from more teachers and students and more classrooms than I can recall, and there isn't room in the pages of this book to give them all due credit even if I could. Additionally, you'll see that the student writing included comes from a variety of sources.

A variety of learning models are used. You'll meet over a dozen critical-thinking strategies in the following pages. You are encouraged, also, to bring strategies for writing on demand from other models of learning. The Five Key Practices heighten the rigor of any strategy you found useful in bring your students to new levels of understanding.

Classroom learning "empties" into a connected community. The implication here is, of course, physical, yet *Constructed Responses for Learning* prompts all of students' writing to connect to external sources outside of the texts the students are writing: personal experiences, events, and knowledge of the world events. Student writers explain to their assigned PALs how each entry written connects to
- the writers' experience—text-to-self connection,
- a reading text—text-to-text connection, and
- a current event—text-to-world connection.

Every piece of writing students produce empties into a connected community of the writer.

Learning is personalized by a variety of criteria. In addition to standard expectations of the number of sentences and of key terms, over 15 PALS response strategies allow you to personalize your students' writing to their ability level and learning style. Each PALS strategy populates a toolkit of helpful responses to the quality of each other's writing. As you prompt students to use a variety of PALS strategies in *Constructed Responses for Learning*, you will develop additional PALS strategies of your own and see that some students create viable response strategies themselves.

Assessment is persistent, authentic, transparent, and never punitive. The rubric at the bottom of each journal page fits all four of these conditions. Students can count and assess their use of key terms, sentences, and evidence from tests/lessons, and the wording of the rubric keeps students and their PALs' comments upbeat.

Criteria for success are balanced and transparent. The rubric is the result of extensive testing with thousands of students from a wide range of demographics. It is encouraging to see students use the rubric with ease and see its value, even when some of their teachers do not.

Learning habits are constantly modeled. This means more than "monkey see, monkey do." When you sit and write with your students as they write what you prompt, you dignify writing in your students' minds. They view you as more than a teacher of writing but an actual writer, a doer. My heart thrills every time athletic coaches sit in an ELA, math, science, social studies, or connections class, write with their students, and read it aloud to a typical reaction, "Hey coach, you write that? For real? Wow."

There are constant opportunities for practice. If you want students to reach optimal learning in a course of study, writing constructed responses three times a week is the key. Our classroom action data shows that the pace of three constructed responses a week delivers certain and significant growth in student performance. See www.writingtowin.com/research-based-routines/results/. To support you, *W2W* UNDERSTANDINGS includes 4 to 8 writing prompts for all core standards in ELA, math, science, and social studies. There are more than enough writing prompts for students to meet every day in every class.[2]

Instructional Tools That Support Constructed Responses for Learning

Log of Entries for Teacher Expectations

Whether on a PDF projected on an interactive board or a chart posted on the wall, published expectations for every prompted written entry launches the writing in student journals quite visibly. The Log of Entry that I use (Figure 3.1) includes space for the expectations mentioned in the previous chapter, such as

- Date of the entry
- Number of the entry
- Number of sentences
- Number of key terms
- Description of the writing prompt
- The letter of the critical-thinking strategy

Figure 3.1 Log of Entries for Teacher Expectations

Log of Entries for Teacher Expectations

Beginning date _____
Ending date _____

STRATEGY			
A—What I Thought You Taught	F—Memory Sentence	J—Sentence Expansion	
B—Acrostic Vocabulary	G—Copy and Continue	K—Free Writing	
C—Either . . . Or	H—Change the tense/number/point of view	L—Analogy	
D—Focused Free Writing	I—Admit Slip	M—Miscellaneous	
E—Quad Cluster			

Date	Entry	Teacher expects	# of key terms	Description of writing prompt	Strategy
8–13	1	5–6 sentences	5–6	I am (fill in the blank), the mathematician.	D
8–15	2	5–6 sentences	5–6	I am (fill in the blank), the geometrician.	D
8–17	3	6–7 facts	5–6	ABSOLUTE (value) _____ .	B
8–20	4	5–6 sentences	5–6	. . . what I have learned about computing unit rates using ratios._____	I
8–21	5	6–7 facts	5–6	ORDER OF OPERATIONS .	B
8–23	6	5–6 sentences	5–6	Explain with examples situations where you need to use variables _____ .	D
8–26	7	4–6 sentences	5–6	interest, gratuity, percent*, fraction _____	E
8–27	8	5–6 sentences	5–6	Which is easier to calculate, the amount of a tip on a dinner bill or a return on an investment in the stock market? _____	C
8–28	9	5–6 sentences	5–6	easier, finding the square root or cube root?	C
8–29	10	5–7 sentences	5–6	Explain with examples how the square of a number is the number times itself _____ .	D
9–3	11	3–5 sentences	5–6	square root : square :: factor : product	L
9–5	12	4–6 sentences	5–6	guess, approximate, calculate*, hypothesize _____	E
9–6	13	3–5 sentences	5–6	tip : percentage :: first half : portion of a game _____ .	L

eRESOURCES

Of course, you need not use my Log of Entries, but I find including the six features of teacher expectations is non-negotiable. Undoubtedly, it is more than some practiced writers need, but it does not offend them, and it nurtures less confident writers in their practice. The power of teachers tracking student expectations and students tracking their progress in course learning has been thoroughly established through viable research.

A corresponding Log of Entries for Student Self-check (Figure 3.2) makes sure that students track their individual progress throughout a course of study.

Note how a student tracks all six features of teacher expectations set by her teacher. It's imperative that students be coached to record and then be held accountable for recording all six on every constructed response they write.

A Three-Part Rubric for Self-Assessment

The three-part rubric for self-assessment is very simple. A plus (+) shows that the students believe they exceeded your expectations. A target (◉) shows that they met expectations. A rectangle (▭) claims that they approached the expectations.

Focus Board for Writing

Whatever feature of the curriculum gets serious wall space sets the tone in a learning environment. To secure the significant gains for your student performance like those in our Action Research reports, ensure that all classrooms post and maintain a focus board for writing.

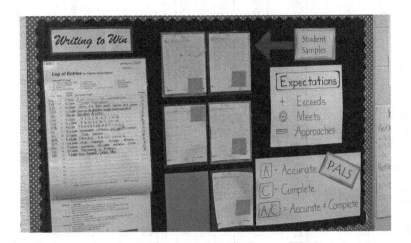

Pyramid of Average Retention Rates of Learning

Since writing as a major venue for learning is not widely practiced in the US, this chart[3] serves as a constant reminder of the reason "Why we write to learn."

Figure 3.2 Log of Entries for Student Self-check

Log of Entries for Student Self-check

STRATEGY			Beginning date _____
			Ending date _____
A—What I Thought You Taught		F—Memory Sentence	J—Sentence Expansion
B—Acrostic Vocabulary		G—Copy and Continue	K—Free Writing
C—Either...Or		H—Change the tense/number/point of view	L—Analogy
D—Focused Free Writing		I—Admit Slip	M—Miscellaneous
E—Quad Cluster			

Date	Entry	Teacher expects	Self-check	# of key terms / Description of writing prompt	Strategy
8-13	1	5–6 sentences	+	5–6 T / I am (fill in the blank), the mathematician.	D
8-15	2	5–6 sentences	◉	5–6 T / I am (fill in the blank), the geometrician.	D
8-17	3	6–7 facts	◉	5–6 T / ABSOLUTE (value)	B
8-20	4	5–6 sentences	+	5–6 T / ... what I have learned about computing unit rates using ratios.	I
8-21	5	6–7 facts	+	5–6 T / ORDER OF OPERATIONS	B
8-23	6	5–6 sentences	+	5–6 T / Explain with examples situations where you use variables.	D
8-26	7	4–6 sentences	+	5–6 T / interest, gratuity, percentage, fraction*	E
8-27	8	5–6 sentences	+	5–6 T / Which is easier to calculate, the amount of a tip on a dinner bill or a return on an investment in the stock market?	C
8-28	9	5–6 sentences	+	5–6 T / easier, finding the square root or cube root?	C
8-29	10	5–7 sentences	◉	5–6 T / Explain with examples how the square of a number is the number times itself	D
9-3	11	3–5 sentences	◉	5–6 T / square root : square :: factor : product.	L
9-5	12	4–6 sentences	◉	5–6 T / guess, approximate, calculate, hypothesize	E
9-6	13	3–5 sentences	+	5–6 T / tip : percent :: first half : portion of a game.	L

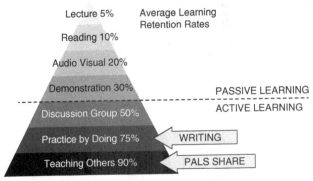

Lecture 5%

Average Learning
Retention Rates

Reading 10%

Audio Visual 20%

Demonstration 30%

PASSIVE LEARNING

ACTIVE LEARNING

Discussion Group 50%

Practice by Doing 75%

WRITING

Teaching Others 90%

PALS SHARE

Source: National Training Laboratories, Bethel, Maine

These percents derive from the research of Edgar Dale; however, Dale cautions readers not to take the assigned percentages literally.[4] It is rare that any lesson is delivered exclusively in one of these modes of learning. That's good advice for interpreting and applying any data delivered in percents. Nonetheless, the percents do make solid intuitive sense. We retain less of new knowledge that we hear than what we view audiovisually. Further, the knowledge acquired early in our K-12 schooling that we remember today is often the outcome of projects or written reports (practice by doing). The difference between the effectiveness of active learning (the bottom three levels) and passive learning (the top four levels) is obvious and noteworthy. Certainly, the overall force of these numbers underscores the power of writing to learn and explains how students can best act with other invested learners.

For this reason, in every school I train teachers, the administrators receive one of these charts to post in the school's data room, and all of the administrators take turns explaining how the pyramid explains, "Why we use **writing** to learn!"

Picture Makers and Picture Killers

Of the three traits—mental voice, pictures, and flow—pictures is the trait on which to place greatest emphasis. After all, it is the trait that receives greater weight on state and national writing rubrics. Fortunately, it is also the easiest of the three for students to understand, identify, and use. So many times, I simply say in response to the writing of a student PAL of mine, "I just don't see a clear picture here yet." Invariably he/she pulls out a pencil and busily adds in details that make the picture appear in my mind. For these reasons, it is important to give students a leg up on how best to enhance the mental pictures in their writing.

Writing research shows that function words (prepositions and conjunctions) are the most effective words for elaborating thought with mental pictures. Some textbooks define adjectives and adverbs as words that add details to writing.

While this is true, adding a good number of adjectives and adverbs to a sentence makes it appear contrived. An elementary student produced this descriptive sentence in a first draft.

A big, bright red, yellow striped, round ball became the life of the party.

When given the opportunity to use picture makers in revision, he came up with a sentence that made him smile.

A big round <u>ball</u> that was bright red <u>with</u> yellow stripes became the life of the party.

Or as this teacher model for secondary students shows an original sentence

The gentleman approached the Atlanta Hilton Hotel bar.

Adding details exclusively with adjectives and adverbs, a student produced

The <u>slight-built, mustachioed, Mayberry-born, 85-year-old</u> gentleman <u>reluctantly</u> approached <u>the highly polished, elegant, downtown maple</u> Atlanta Hilton Hotel bar.

Sole reliance on adjectives and adverbs moves beyond cumbersome to confusing. A teacher served the same sentence up with nine Picture Makers (allowing her to add an image of a twisted mustache).

The slight-built gentleman, <u>who</u> was born <u>in</u> Mayberry over 85 years ago, <u>twisted</u> one end <u>of</u> his mustache <u>as</u> he approached the elegant bar <u>of</u> highly polished maple <u>in</u> the Hilton Hotel of downtown Atlanta <u>with</u> reluctance.

Use of an expected number of Picture Makers leads to interesting and energetic word choices that surprise the writer as well as engage and even delight the readers.

Picture Makers

about	around	below/beneath
above	as	beside(s)
across	aside	between
after	at	beyond
against	atop	but
along	because	by
amid(st)	before	concerning
among(st)	behind/below	despite

down	near	through(out)
during	next	under(neath)
except	on	unlike
following	of	until
for	off	up(on)
from	out(side)	when
given	over	which
in(to)	since	who
including	than	with(in/out)
inside	that	yet
like	to(ward)	

On the other hand, it is a decent idea to also place a list of words that bring pictures back to the writer's mind but do little to convey those detailed pictures to the minds of their readers. On prominent display alongside of the Picture Makers chart, the Picture Killers chart provides students an easy reference to use in re-reading their constructed responses. Students find it natural to replace picture killers with words or phrases to enhance the pictures. Together, these wall charts provide a quite student-friendly pair of resources.

Picture Killers
(except in dialogue of characters)

a bit (a lot)	cool	go (went)
all	cute	good
area	deal	great
awesome	do (did)	guy
be (is, was)	dude	have (had)
bad	eat (ate) everything	here
big	fine	hit
beautiful	fixing to	hot
came	get	know (knew)
can (would)	give	kind of

let	see	thing
like (love)	so	truly
made	some	try
nice	somehow	very
neat	somewhat	want
person	sort (of)	weird
pretty	start (to)	well
put	stuff	will (would)
really	super	you know
say (said)	take	
scary	there	

Summing Up

Interactive learning logs of constructed responses (as opposed to diaries or journals) assure that a system of composing constructed responses does not operate in a vacuum. They ensure that writing is a part of the larger design of a highly effective classroom environment. Essential characteristics include making sure that

- questions are valued over answers,
- ideas come from divergent sources,
- a variety of learning models is used,
- classroom learning "empties" into a connected community,
- learning is personalized by a variety of criteria,
- assessment is persistent, authentic, transparent, and never punitive,
- criteria for success are balanced and transparent,
- learning habits are constantly modeled, and
- there are constant opportunities for practice.

The instructional tools that support these characteristics and the Five Key Practices of chapter 2 include

- Log of Entries for Teacher Expectations
- Log of Entries for Student Self-check
- The three-part rubric for self-assessment
- Focus Board for Writing
- Pyramid of Average Retention Rates of Learning
- Picture Makers and Picture Killers

Looking Ahead

The next section turns to practical critical-thinking strategies that ensure engagement in analyzing new knowledge from reading texts and class lessons at a range of depths of knowledge. It offers a viable answer to a critical question. What instructional tools and procedures in classroom instruction make the best use of the Five Key Practices of writing-based learning?

Notes

1. D.J. MacAulay (1990), "Classroom Environment: A Literature Review." *Educational Psychology* 10(3) 239–253; T.V. Savage, *Teaching Self Control through Management and Discipline*, 1999.
2. Terry Heick, www.teachthought.com/learning/10-characteristics-of-a-highly-effective-learning-environment/
3. Pyramid of Average Learning Retention Rates, released by the US Department of Education (DOE), 1981.
4. E. Dale and J. S. Chall (1948). "A Formula for Predicting Readability." *Educational Research Bulletin* 27(11): 20–28.

Section II

Critical-Thinking Strategies That Fine-Tune Constructed Responses for Emerging and Independent Writers

Chapter 4

Something on the Page That Helps You Remember What You Were Thinking
(Letters, Words, Phrases, Numbers, Symbols, or Drawings)

"All my students believe they can write when they come to me," said a kindergarten teacher, Miss Robinson, to a group of student teachers I supervised early on in my career. "Most of them have been punished for writing on walls or on pages of books of checkbook registers. What makes many of them anxious is learning to read."

"That's not real writing, right?" quipped one of the students.

"That's a fair question," she responded. "It takes us right to the point. The first day of school, I tell the students that 'writing is putting marks on paper that help you remember what you are thinking.' This definition helps students know when they are writing and when they need to keep practicing."

"You mean it doesn't matter if students use letters and words when they write?"

"That's right. Of course, a few of them write words and sentences from day one; the rest watch these few very carefully."

"Don't the ones who can't write letters and words, uh, feel bad?"

"Not if they can remember what they were thinking when they drew or scribbled or borrowed words. That's another really good question," complimented the teaching veteran. "Let's all have a seat at this large table in the back of the room, and I may answer most of your questions before you ask."

She and I both knew she would.

The Remember Game for Emerging Writers

As she had with several student groups before, Miss R passed out a clean sheet of unlined paper to each student teacher seated around the expansive workspace.

"Follow my directions and you'll see exactly how writing is the ultimate differentiator. It prompts all my kindergartners to trust what they are thinking."

She directed students to draw a line from the top center of the page to the bottom and a line from center left side of the page to the right side. She showed what she had drawn as she directed them. Her page was divided into four equal quadrants.

"Nice," she encouraged all who had created quadrants on their pages. "Now, place a tiny *1* in the corner of the box like I have" and showed them all a small number one in the corner of the upper left quadrant, "We'll call this Box 1." She continued to show them how to number all four boxes, "Now, put some marks in Box 1 that helps you remember the story we've read, 'The Little Red Hen.'" Miss R shielded her writing, but the students could see she was modeling what she wanted them to do—write what they were thinking.

As always, the student teachers wrote exactly as directed.

The Little Red Hen

with uppercase letters on each word like the title. Miss R showed them her page that had only one word in Box 1, three uppercase letters

RED

"I *borrowed* the word *red* from the science word board on the cupboard by the sink," she said as she gestured to the random arrangement of words around a color wheel behind the students.

"Now, here's how the game proceeds. I direct them to place marks in the other three boxes that help them remember phrases from our study together:

Three happy ghosts [It was just two weeks until Halloween.]
The birthday circle [Juan's mother brought cupcakes for his birthday today.]
It's raining outside [Indeed, it was, a fact indicated on the weather board.]

Miss R let me and the students write what we heard in boxes 1–3. She wrote the number *three*, the words *birthday* and *rain* in the boxes on her page. She held up what she had written and assessed the writing of the student teachers, "I see you have done as well as my kindergartners. Of course, it takes them ten minutes to write what took us about one, and they would include some nice drawings to elaborate on their thoughts and impress their teacher. I can see that didn't cross your minds." The students laughed as they looked at one another.

"Now it's time for student self-assessment," she announced as she stood and walked to a side bulletin board. "Here is our writing focus board. It's the board that guides and stores our writing progress. As you can see it includes the Log of Entries (see p. 33) where I log a description of what we write and a place for us to post student exemplars for the nine patterns of writing development."

"My students know that the minute they finish writing, they self-assess. For kindergarten, that means placing the number of the pattern that their writing resembles. I've already assessed my writing as a "5" since I borrowed all of the words I wrote from around the room: *RED* from the science word board, *THREE* from the math board, *HAPPY* and *BIRTHDAY* from the language boards, and *RAIN* from the science board."

"Check out the nine patterns posted here, and decide which fits what you have written in your four boxes," she guided the students through the nine patterns in the following way.

Picture Maker (1)—This writer spends his time on his art, then when he explains his work, he says what the picture brings to his mind at the moment. It is likely a different story each time.

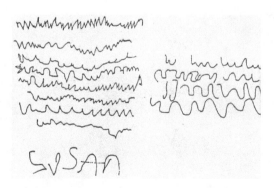

Scribbler (2)—This writer has determined that writing is different from art. She mimics what she has seen older folks do as they write. She has even shown me her writing and asks me to read it for her. The best thing to do in this case is to ask what she was thinking when she was writing.

Verbal Story Teller (3)—In contrast to Pattern 1, this artist is more concerned about meaning than art. He tells a version of the same story each time he presents his writing to others.

Letter Shaker (4)—The writer of Pattern 4 shows a connection between the illustration and the letters. She writes letters from left to right; her story remains constant, but it may be due more to the illustration than the writing.

Borrower (5)—I demonstrated this pattern of writing in my model as I wrote with you. I borrowed a word from word walls and placed them on my paper, thinking they would help me remember all I'd said. It may not, but my story will remain the same. Borrowers know words are important in remembering writing and remembering their thoughts.

Sound Maker (6)—Moving beyond borrowing, this writer sounds out words she chooses to write with her illustrations. Since letter formation is tedious, few words actually appear. They may not be easily deciphered by others. This pattern is a critical hurdle for many kindergartners who suddenly worry about spelling, but you see, I haven't, and don't, mention the word spelling in writing. It's just borrowing.

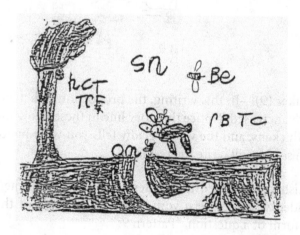

Labeler (7)—This writer is my budding Richard Scarry. She must feel compelled to label each feature of her illustration, writing quickly to provide all of the help that she can.

Sentence Maker (8)—This writer appears to have it all together and represents his thoughts in single sentences. When I ask him what more there is to the story, he gives me a look like *What don't you understand? I wrote the story.* He may even read it again, this time a bit slower and louder for my benefit.

Story Maker (9)—In this writing, the proportion of letters to illustration has greatly increased. Notice the story line in these two sentences; the plot actually thickens, and the writer gladly tells you what happened next. He may even say he will write the rest later.

As Miss R finished, she asked the student teachers, "Well, there you have it; have you decided which pattern your writing fits?" One of them tentatively offered in the form of a question, "Pattern 9?"

"I know why you would think so, but let me be clear that none of you wrote sentences, so your writing is neither Patterns 8 nor 9. If you believe you borrowed what you wrote from me, your writing is Pattern 5. More likely, you labeled each box as I directed you, Pattern 7."

One student raised her hand, "But none of us are emerging writers. None of these patterns really fit us."

"How right you are," replied Miss R, "You all write much beyond Pattern 9, I know. Yet what you wrote today was at best Pattern 7. Who can explain what I mean?"

"I think I can," volunteered another student, "The context affects the way we write. You told us to label four boxes, and we did as you asked; that's Pattern 7."

"Exactly," smiled Miss R, "Well said. And my kindergartners see that adults sometimes use one of the nine patterns even in their own writing. ELA teachers call them fragments and say something like 'It's OK for professional writers to use fragments.' What I show my kindergartners is that everybody uses fragments when they work just fine."

Miss R presented the lesson well once again. I often wondered if the power of context in writing stuck with my student teachers. I hoped so since it took Miss R's lesson to remind me what I had learned in a *Sociology of Language* course in my graduate studies. The stresses of a pre-tenured educator seemed to blur what was important.

Remember Game Exemplars from Emerging Writers

Acrostic Vocabulary for Independent Writers

The Remember Game presents differently for independent writers, so it goes by a different name—Acrostic Vocabulary. The Acrostic Vocabulary strategy focuses on remembering what students learned from a lesson, not just what they were thinking. Using writing to learn is the important next step after students understand that writing helps them remember what they were thinking. Additionally, when students recall the expected number of facts about a course concept, they often have an "ah-hah" moment when they induce the fullness of the concept from its detailed facts.

Acrostic Vocabulary is foundational to all of the other strategies. Mastering an acrostic response conditions students to the mental rigor needed in the rest of the writing they do in courses of study. An Acrostic Vocabulary prompt

- connects students' writing directly back to the facts and details of concepts they were taught,
- encourages them to use excerpts of what they were taught,
- requires them to re-configure the facts in their own words, and
- does not impose the rules of Standard Written English on their writing.

It goes without saying that when students put what they have been taught in their own words, it counts as evidence that they have learned it. The guidelines from the "Guide for Writing to Learn" read like this:

1. Write the assigned word(s) down the page, one letter per line.
2. Write a fact of four words or more about the word(s), beginning the first word of each fact with the letter on each line.

3. Use only facts that are different from each other.
4. You may not use the words(s) you are defining.

The Acrostic Vocabulary strategy is all about spotting a key fact from a lesson or reading text and making sure that your version of the fact represents the fact with precision. As with all strategies for constructed response, the Five Key Practices apply. For the acrostic, the practices look like this.

	Key Practice	Description
1	Quantify your expectations for each constructed response.	Quantify the number of key terms and facts you expect students to use in their response to every acrostic you prompt. • Note that the number of key terms are in addition to the word(s) they are defining. • Expect 5–6 facts for grade 4–8 students even though the assigned word(s) include 7 or more letters. From the first acrostic, emphasize that students are responsible for only 5–6 facts, even in words like *photosynthesis, introduction,* or *constitution.*
2	Write your own personal response to Acrostic Vocabulary prompts the first couple of times.	Provide your model response to the prompt that you assigned to students. Even if they echo your model, they are practicing a response that follows the "Guide for Writing to Learn" (see eResources). The structure of your response to the acrostic is novel to them, and attempting to parrot what they heard you read accelerates their awareness and mastery of the strategy. Make sure your model exceeds your expectations of student responses.
3	Guide student choices with a simple critical-thinking strategy.	All students read aloud the guidelines in the "Guide for Writing to Learn" for Strategy B. A choral reading of the four guidelines documents that students are engaged in thought about the strategy. **Note:** Acrostics are written by two Acrostic Buddies until students show they can exceed your expectations on their own.
4	Prompt specific PALS strategies with each entry	Using only the strategy you assign, PALs complete the following sentence stem, "The strength of your writing is. . . ." An acrostic entry is most often in the informational genre.
5	Secure student self-assessment.	When students finish their entries, they complete the three-pronged self-assessment. 1. "I used key terms with meaning." 2. "I wrote meaningful facts." 3. "I used evidence from parts of the text or lesson." Students then read their entries aloud to a person other than their Acrostic Buddies and show, in their writing, evidence of their three scores. PALs confirm (√) or question (?) each score.

When you prompt students to construct responses using the Acrostic Vocabulary strategy, present them with words or phrases of a topic that

- are foundational to the study of a course topic,
- contain 2 or more letters than the number of facts you expect, and
- require several key terms to describe them fully.

When you present foundational terms for all acrostic prompts, you will

- find it easier to write a model entry yourself, and
- create acrostics that divulge more about what your students understand,
- . . . and misunderstand.

By the same token, students will

- respond to the prompts more readily,
- find the prompts easier to analyze and interpret,
- write explanations that are

  o easier for students to process, and
  o more likely to stay with them,

- recast the vocabulary in ways that boosts deeper understanding,
- develop a critical-thinking habit to use the rest of their lives, and
- satisfy their innate desire to know more.

When students work with a buddy to meet your expectations for responding to acrostics and explaining their new knowledge to PALs, expect the terms to show up with precision in class discussions and written class reports. You may notice that they interpret test items that contain these terms more readily. You'll see students with increased control over the language of the content area.

So as you look for ways of employing the Acrostic Vocabulary strategy for activating or summarizing key concepts in learning, consider the following techniques that have worked well for other teachers:

- Begin with acrostics defined by key terms found in a glossary or text recently experienced by your students. Students, then, extract facts and rephrase them before they plug them in their entries.
- Let students complete a foundational term like *landforms* in one day.

  o In place of a PALS response strategy, field facts for each letter from the class to help the class form the most insightful entry possible.
  o On the second day, randomly assign specific landforms to the acrostic buddies such as *coastal plain, isthmus, lagoon, marsh, peninsula, piedmont,* and *plateau.*

Exemplars of Acrostic Entries for and from Independent Writers

Intermediate Grades

At the conclusion of a unit on geometric shapes, Johnston's math teacher let small groups select from a number of math terms and create a group acrostic. His group settles on POLYGONS, and his version turned out quite different the rest of his PALs.

Prompt: *POLYGONS*

Key terms: *angles, closed shape, congruent, hexagon, inside angles, irregular, octagon, pentagon, plan, point, quadrilaterals, regular, straight lines, triangle, two dimensions*

Expectations: 5–6 key terms; 5–6 facts

> P–entagons have five congruent sides.
> O–ctagons have eight congruent sides.
> L–ines must be straight.
> Y–ou see angles inside them and outside them.
> G–ot to have at least three angles
> O–nly includes closed shapes
> N–
> S–ame number of angles and sides

— Johnston H, grade 4

Later Grades

Tatiana's biology teacher prompted student response with the Acrostic Vocabulary strategy often. The overwhelming number of new vocabulary introduced in the course makes it a logical choice. As a separate task that each person selected, she chose the human brain and found a reading text at Frontiers for Young Minds (http://kids.frontiersin.org/article/10.3389/frym.2014.00006).

Prompt: *HUMAN BRAIN*

Key terms: *20%, anesthesia, associating, brain cells, change hearing, change sight, consciousness, involuntary, ongoing, movement, nerve center, ripples, sensation, wander*

Expectations: 5–6 key terms; 5–6 facts

H-ealthy means <u>ongoing</u> hard-working <u>cells</u>.

U-

M-uch like the heart, its work is <u>involuntary</u>.

A-nesthesia stops <u>consciousness</u>, <u>movement</u> and <u>sensation</u>, not other activity

N-o other animal has a <u>nerve center</u> as complex

B-roadcasts and receives message from the whole body

R-

A-lways alters the way we <u>hear</u> and <u>see</u>

I-

N-o cells die; they only get lazy when we don't use them

— Tatiana S, grade 10

Typically, acrostics do contain short facts, often just parts of a sentence. One middle school teacher saw the acrostic as an opportunity to ask students to bring closure to their understanding of the topic prompted. Gabriel provides a solid exemplar of this twist on the strategy.

Prompt: *SELMA*

Key terms: *outlawed blacks, voting rights, NAACP, Jim Crowe Laws, bridge, organized, segregation, Martin Luther King, Jr., lawsuits*

Expectations: 5–6 key terms; 4–5 facts

S-outher states <u>outlawed blacks</u> from places in public and their <u>voting rights</u>.

E-qual rights were not extended to blacks so they formed a solution, the <u>NAACP</u>

L-awsuits threatened if blacks did not follow the Jim Crowe Laws.

M-any blacks and even whites marched without violence on the bridge into town.

A-ssassinated at 39 years old, Martin Luther King, Jr. no longer led, but his teaching still lives on.

— Gabriel C, grade 8

Colby finds that writing helps him "wrap his mind" around a topic. His Acrostic entry illustrates what he means. His list-writing style does show that he is pulling chunks of new knowledge into five detailed facts.

Prompt: *CHINA'S HISTORY*

Key terms: *Mao Zedong, communism, industrialization, famine, nationalists, civil war, Shanghai, dictator, cultural revolution, People's Republic of China*

Expectations: 6–7 key terms, 6–8 facts

C-ommunism brought by Mao Zedong

H-e (Mao) led the long march of 6000 kilometers.

I-ndustrialization (Great Leap Forward) was a disaster.

N-ationalists fought the communists in a civil war and retreated to and island (Taiwan).

A-lot of people starved in one of the greatest famines during the revolution.

S-hanghai still became the commercial center of East China. Beijing was Mao's capital.

H-e (Deng Xiaoping) was second dictator with quotes, "Keep a cool head and maintain a low profile. Never take the lead but aim at doing something."

I-

S-

T-iananmen Square (1989)-killed protesters became a battle cry for more revolution

O-ctober 1st, 1949 marks the 1st day of People's Republic of China.

R-

Y-es, Mao did make his citizens carry a book of his speeches with them everywhere.

— Colby J, grade 7

Acrostics and Course Standards

A second progression for creating acrostics serves to increases students' depth and breadth of knowledge. It expands their awareness of connection between writing what they have just learned to

- a concept in a previous lesson or another subject area;
- facts already known from everyday life; and
- observations about the world beyond their families, neighborhood, or community.

Early Grades

Acrostics within a Single Standard

It is easy to vary the acrostics drawn on terms from within a standard. It is customary to start with foundation concepts like *opinion, geometry, genetics*, and *landforms* like in the following table. As a follow-up to flesh out the details of the standard, assign the remaining terms to small groups. The end of the journal writing includes each group presenting its acrostic to the class.

Subject	Standard	Acrostic prompts
ELA	Introduce a topic or text clearly, state an opinion, and create an organizational structure in which related ideas are grouped to support the writer's purpose.	OPINION—ALTERNATE CLAIM, REASONS, LOGICAL
Math	Recognize and draw shapes having specified attributes, such as a given number of angles or a given number of equal faces. Identify triangles, quadrilaterals, pentagons, hexagons, and cubes.	GEOMETRY—TRIANGLES, PARALLEL, DIMENSION
Science	Students will recognize how biological traits are passed on to successive generations.	GENETICS— BREEDING, INHERIT, REPRODUCTION
Social studies	The student will locate important places in the United States.	LANDFORMS— PLATEAUS, DESERTS, CANYONS, PENINSULA

Acrostics across Standards or Subject Areas

When you begin including terms from more than one standard, the acrostic prompts students to increased depth of knowledge. A model acrostic written by an elementary school teacher demonstrates her expectation for an acrostic that contrasts and compare plants and animals.

How Plants Differ from Animals

P—rovide food and oxygen for animals
L—eaves produce food, but animals consume food
A—flower is like the adults in animals
N—o walking, swimming or flying, just roots for standing and taking in minerals and water
T—he stem holds the arteries and veins instead a body
S—tudied by botanists instead of zoologists

A middle school science teacher offers a similar model for an Acrostic Vocabulary entry.

How Mammals Differ from Crustaceans

M—ammalogists study them instead of carcinologists

A—n internal vs. external skeleton

M—ore organs for digestion are needed

M—oulting is not necessary

A—family life instead of a school

L—ead food into their mouths with tongues, lips and teeth instead of
mandibles and maxillas

S—ense their surroundings with ears and nose instead of antennae

Acrostics Related to Everyday Life

The interesting insights that show up in acrostics when students relate new
knowledge or course standards to everyday life ranges from mundane to surprising, even mysterious. One thing is certain. The connection that the acrostic has helped them make to the standard solders the new knowledge in their
minds indelibly, and it could last them a lifetime.

Subject	Standard	Acrostic Prompts
ELA	Introduce a topic or text clearly, state an opinion, and create an organizational structure in which related ideas are grouped to support the writer's purpose.	Strong opinions— BEDTIMES, DRESSCODE, HOMEWORK
Math	Recognize and draw shapes having specified attributes, such as a given number of angles or a given number of equal faces. Identify triangles, quadrilaterals, pentagons, hexagons, and cubes.	Geometric shapes in— BUILDINGS, SKYLINES, LANDFORMS
Science	Classify organisms based on physical characteristics using a dichotomous key of the six kingdom system (archaebacteria, eubacteria, protists, fungi, plants, and animals).	Organism in—PUBLIC PARK, NEIGHBORHOOD, STREAMS, FRESH-WATER (ponds) / LAGOONS
Social studies	The student will locate important places in the United States.	Landforms on—FIELD TRIP, VACATION (spot), BIKE RIDE

Benefits Teachers Attribute to the Use of the Remember Game and Acrostics

These two strategies have extraordinary impact on emerging writers (Remember Game) and independent writers (Acrostic Vocabulary) who are meeting
challenging new information. They both start at the most accessible level possible for students. They, in fact, nudge them into early successes in writing from
the first day of writing constructed responses for learning.

- The Remember Game

  - Provides hands-on experience with putting something on paper that helps them remember what they were thinking. Eventually, students realize that remembering our thoughts is what is all important in writing.
  - "Never thought I'd see the day learning to write helped students read with confidence. This is the third year I've seen it happen with my slowest learners." (South Dakota public school teacher)
  - "My students don't even realize they are working hard at writing. When their writing looks like Pattern 8, they tell me it's ready to hang on the wall." (North Carolina Montessori school teacher)
  - "Until the Remember Game, I never thought all kindergartners could start writing in the first days of school." (Georgia public school teacher)
  - "The Remember Game gives my special needs writers and my gifted ones a real sense of accomplishment. Amazing!" (Mississippi parochial school teacher)

- The Acrostic Vocabulary strategy

  - Provides hands-on practice with reconfiguring the language of a lesson or text in students' own words.
  - "Acrostics are the bridge strategy between my emerging and independent writers. I buddy an emerging writer with an independent writer, and soon there are two independent writers." (Georgia public school teacher)
  - "Acrostics are my students' favorite strategy. They jot down insights at DOK 2 and DOK 3 on a daily basis." (South Dakota private school teacher)
  - "Acrostics are my son's favorite because he doesn't have to write sentences. They are mine because they let me see his deepest insights into key vocabulary of course standards." (North Carolina home-school teacher)
  - "Acrostics help students break the complex terms of auto mechanics into meaningful facts. I'm stunned by how quickly they learn the course vocabulary." (South Carolina public school teacher)
  - "Acrostics lay the foundation for learning at the beginning of lessons. I recommend them to all my beginning teachers who don't see how to get their students to write." (Georgia public school principal)

- A favorite strategy of students,

  - Teachers report that acrostics show up unassigned. Once students bring the first one in from home, others follow the lead.
  - They think that they are easy and fun.

    - The facts don't have to be complete sentences.
    - They are allowed to work with a buddy.

- They can use a glossary or reading text to find the "answers."
- Acrostics match emerging writers' habit of inductive thinking.
- Students feel intelligent when reading their acrostics aloud to a PAL.

- Builds on the innate propensity of students to label objects, animals, and plants in the groups they place them.
- A sure way to vault students' minds into higher-order thinking in a matter of minutes.

Summing Up

Seen as a pair, the Remember Game and Acrostic Vocabulary strategies provide firm foundations for launching routines of constructed responses for learning. The Remember Game boldly asks students to *write* anything that helps them remember what you have asked them to remember. It requires your patience as you accept without judgment some students' obvious misunderstanding. Acrostic Vocabulary lures independent writers into attempting to rephrase new knowledge that would otherwise be impenetrable. In trekking towards new understanding a foreign concept, they are strengthened by working with a PAL to list key facts, not well-structured sentences. The outcome is often an "Ah-hah" when they reread their acrostic about a term like *osmosis* and realize that there is nothing mystical about molecules moving from an area of high concentration to one of lower concentration. It is no different than a person leaving an overcrowded room to go outside and "get some fresh air." With the aid of these two strategies, students can move to the next strategies with the confidence of fluent thinkers and writers.

Suggested Readings

Toby Fulwiler, *The Journal Book,* 1989.
Sepideh Sadaghiani, "The Brain Never Stops," Frontiers for Young Minds, http://kids.frontiersin.org/article/10.3389/frym.2014.00006

Chapter 5

Free Writing Rigorous Thought

Keep your pencils moving!

Write anything that comes to your mind!

If you can't think of anything to write, write "I can't think of anything to write."

Trust your thoughts; free writing is a source for many great works of famous, respected authors.

There has always been a place in the ELA strand of the curriculum for free writing, writing that is a free association of ideas on a topic or topics that students have been taught thoroughly. For emerging writers, however, a guided strategy accelerates their journey into exploring their own thoughts. There is no better launch of free writing than the Sentence Stems strategy. For independent writers, their free writing needs a focus, hence the name of the strategy, Focused Free Writing.

Quick Writes That Show What Students Are Learning!

Quick writes have had a long and quite varied life over the last four decades. When I first met them, they served as a way for me to get my thoughts moving; later they helped develop fluency of thought; soon, I was a much more fluent thinker in writing than I have ever become in personal or public conversation. My personal experience with quick writes has been positive and productive. Unfortunately, quick writes are too often perceived by students and teachers alike as writing without restraint. Such writing can have its place, but this chapter presents a different take on quickly written free writing. Free writing with a standards-based focus can and, indeed, needs to disclose students' deepest thoughts on a topic of importance in a course of study.

Sentence Stems as Free Writing for Emerging Writers

In her classic 1970 book, *The Art of Teaching Writing*, Lucy Calkins sets the first expectations for student writing by grade level for elementary and middle school years. Although long out of print, the book still perches in a hallowed spot on my office shelves and serves as a guide, second to none, in the positioning of writing prompts for students. Chapter 4, entitled "First Grade: An Era of Confidence," describes first graders whom she studied in the mid-1960s much like the first graders I see in the schools I serve each year. Much research in the teaching of reading and writing has transpired since this landmark publication, but little of it has improved on the basic understanding of how writing develops and is best supported. Oh, the student exemplars have changed, but the characterization of mental and social development related to growth in writing remains remarkably constant.

Calkins cites as evidence of this era the confidence when first grade students use repeated sentence patterns with complete satisfaction with the nature and impact of their writing on an audience. Still wrapped in ego-centric thought (à la Jean Piaget), these emerging writers eagerly show what they know and write a list of sentences for anyone who will stop and watch them in action.

At first, the Sentence Stem strategy amounts to an opportunity for students to show off all the words they have mastered (spelled and almost spelled). Aiko's entry is a good example.

I like mom.
I like dad.
I like mi litel sitr. [little sister]
I like red.
I like green.
I like yellow.
I like plaig hows. [playing house]
I like bedes. [beads]
I like julry. [jewelry]
I like prite clos. [pretty clothes]
I like school.
I like Miss Helms.

The week before the US Thanksgiving holiday, Juan wrote, with the aid of the stem, "I see." The first sentence was created by the class as a whole group to model the teacher's expectations. Note how the teacher retains the phonetic spelling that he solicited from the students.

I see a tede ber.
I see a vidow plaer.

I see a tv.
I see a sokr postr.
I see owtsid.
I see
I see so mene thigs.
I am so thankful.

What a solid model of early writing. The entry focused on sight; the topic depended on the mental pictures of the writer. It accepted invented spellings, and it ended with a closing sentence that tied it back to the prompt.

As I watched emerging writers rely on written pieces guided completely by sentence stems like *I like, I love, I see, I want,* or *I have,* I realized this was the first evidence of free writing. Yet it was not constrained by a focus on an idea. It occurred in the writing development of a majority of newly acclaimed independent writers, as early as late kindergarten and late as the first of second grade. It was as if they grabbed onto a stem that gave them a way to show off all of the ideas in school that they had mastered.

How long students' writing continued as a jot list of sentences with words they could sound out was impossible to predict. Then I remembered the answer forwarded by Piaget. These writers of sentence stems will continue to rely on them exclusively for their writing as long as they believe the strategy works. And the lists of sentence stems continue as long as the student writers perceive that the lists show

- Evidence of acceptable writing to them
- That an audience views a draft of completed sentence stems as acceptable writing
- They see the stem conveys what they are thinking fully

Primary grade students insert other sentence patterns as they follow the pattern of one sentence stem as they realize

- The need to explain more about one of their completed sentence stems.

I have a tede bar.
I have a litl brothr.
I have a futball.
I have a soccer gol.
It is big.
But it has a hole in it.
A ball cun skor.
I have lots a stuf.

- Questions or pushback from their PALs or significant adults (parents, grandparents, family friends, or other teachers). I've observed one PAL responding to a Sentence Stem writer with honesty and precision, "Is that how you write? It's just a list." or "Who told you to write like that?" or even a statement like, "I don't think that counts as writing."

Whatever the case, as Calkins noted, repeated sentence patterns are one feature of an era of confidence not evident in students' earlier development. And when students are not corrected for writing a list of repetitive sentence patterns, they will write freely with great energy until, as Piaget's theory claims, they see a need to change.

Exemplar of Sentence Stems Entries for and from Emerging Writers

Patience's writing shows how that Sentence Stems lead to independent writing quite naturally. She enjoyed responding to sentence stems often and followed the direction to a "T." Then, it happened, what was supposed to happen. Her sentences began to expand on the stem, go beyond it. The standards focused on plants and animals. On the first day, her writing reviews her class study of plants and animals by listing plants and animal she especially likes.

Prompt: *Plants and Animals I Like . . .*

Expectations: 3–4 key terms, 5–6 sentences

Key terms: *a word wall of 23 plants and animals studied in projects by members of the class.*

> I like robins.
> I like skwirls.
> I like parrots.
> I like cut litel bunnies.
> I like to feed ducks.
> I saw a lion at the zoo.
> I saw a elephant at the zoo.
> I don't like yaks. They are ugly.

On the second day, her teacher invited her to return to her writing and select the one she could write the most about. From the list, it is easy to see why she picked Yaks. Her words show the strongest feelings about them, in this case, negative ones.

> I don't like yaks. They are ugly. You can see one at the zoo. One time I saw a yak at the zoo. It was big and smelly. It got two clos. I love you dady for taeg me to the soo.

Focused Free Writing for Independent Writers

The Focused Free Writing strategy takes Sentence Stems to the next level. Independent writers do more than list possible writing topics. They practice explaining with examples why each topic is important for them to understand. They do write quickly about a new idea; the goal is not to write impressively but to explain fully what they understand. A Focused Free Writing prompt allows students to

- write freely,
- mention examples of what they understand,
- practice citing evidence from lessons or reading texts, and
- focus less on writing skills than content.

It goes without saying that when students put what they have been taught in their own words, it counts as evidence that they have learned it. The guidelines from the "Guide for Writing to Learn" spell it out:

1. Write the prompt at the top of your journal page.
2. Write whatever comes to mind about the prompt using the expected number of key terms provided.
3. Keep your pencil moving, writing your thoughts about the topic until your teacher calls time.

The Focused Free Writing strategy can lose focus unless students explain key facts from a lesson or reading text with evidence from the source. The Five Key Practices deliver the rigor for the strategy.

	Key Practice	Description
I	Quantify your expectations for each constructed response.	Quantify the number of key terms and sentences you expect students to use in their response to every Focused Free Writing prompt that you serve them. • Note that the number of key terms are in addition to the word(s) used in the prompt. • For grade 4–8 students, expect 5–6 key words from a word wall or brainstorm list. • Emphasize the need to refer to more than one part of a lesson or text.
2	Write your own personal response to Focused Free Writing prompts the first couple of times.	Provide your model response to the prompt that you assigned to students. It applies the guidelines for Strategy D, in the "Guide for Writing to Learn" (see eResources). Include unusual examples in your writing; a novel response can stimulate their thinking. Your model writing needs to exceed your expectations of your student responses.

(Continued)

Key Practice	Description
3 Guide student choices with a simple critical-thinking strategy.	All students read aloud the guidelines in the "Guide for Writing to Learn" for Strategy D. A choral reading of the four guidelines documents that students are engaged in thought about the strategy.
4 Prompt specific PALS strategies with each entry.	Using only the strategy you assign, PALs complete the following sentence stem, "The strength of your writing is. . . ." The genre of the Focused Free Writing entry is dictated by the prompt you present.
5 Secure student self-assessment.	When students finish their entries, they complete the three-pronged self-assessment. 1. "I used key terms with meaning." 2. "I wrote meaningful sentences." 3. "I used evidence from parts of the text or lesson." Students then read their entries aloud to a person other than their assigned PALs. PALs confirm (√) or question (?) each assessment.

When you prompt students to construct responses using the Focused Free Writing strategy, provide them with words or phrases on the topic that are directly related to one or more standards of a course of study and require several thoroughly experienced (or taught) key terms to describe fully.

When you provide or brainstorm key terms with a Focused Free Writing prompt, you will

- find it easier to write a model entry yourself, and
- read student entries that divulge more about what they understand,
- . . . and misunderstand.

By the same token, students will

- respond to the prompts more readily,
- write explanations that turn up novel insights,
- use the key terms in their own writing style, and
- develop confidence in presenting their thoughts on demand.

As you look for ways to employ the Focused Free Writing strategy, consider the following techniques that have worked well for other teachers:

- As an alternative to PALs responding in pairs, have students read their entries aloud in groups of 3 or 4 PALs. Prompt PALs to

  o reach consensus on their PALS checks and PALS responses to each other's entries, and
  o select two entries that meet or exceed expectations that are the most different and report to the whole class.

- Divide the class into groups of 6 and assign each group a different topic from the same standard or element of a standard. After completing the Five Key Practices, ask each group to select the most interesting constructed response in their group to share with the class for its response.
- Allow groups of 3 to 5 students to select a key term to explain with examples from a jot list of terms recently studied. Project the list of optional terms and announce that, when one group selects a term, the other groups must choose from those that remain. Allow the small-groups 3 to 5 minutes to jot list 6 to 8 key terms that include 3 or 4 academic words and 3 or 4 domain-specific words (see pp. 165, 170–171, 175).

Exemplars of Focused Free Writing Entries for and from Independent Writers

Early Grades

As a response to the diversity among students in the class, a first grade teacher set up a learning center with resource materials for students to rotate through and read about the customs of their ancestors. Braden read through his resources and looked carefully at each picture. He then placed a silhouette of a Leprechaun in the space at top of his writing paper. He wrote

> I like leprechoun. they are pretty. They <u>dance</u> and <u>wink</u>.
> They are <u>balerins</u>. Joanne is a balenrin and
> Dixie and mary madeline and Wade is nice. He is irish like me
> — Braden M, grade 1

The silhouette is definitely caught in a dance step. On a facing page, a photo of a performance from the Dublin Dance Center seemed to influence his word choice.

In another class, Marcus writes freely about the geometry shapes he sees on his way to school.

Prompt: *Explain with examples what shapes you see around you on your way to school.*

Key terms: *angle, area, circle, geometry, octagon, rectangle, triangle, two dimensions*

Expectations: 4–5 key terms; 5–6 sentences

> On my school bus I get to see all kinds of shapes. I see the shape of <u>rectangles</u> on house doors and windows and <u>triangles</u> make the roof.

Cars ride on four circles. Our bus slows down at an yellow triangles. It is upside down. The driver stops at a red octagon sign. Her steering wheel is a circle. The bus doors are rectangles and they fold open and closed.

— Marcus M, grade 3

Later Grades

The first writing prompt of the year in grade 7 social studies is always "I am _____, the geographer." The teacher asks students to brainstorm key terms, and it is quite clear that the terms derive from all over the science and social studies curriculum. To be sure, a number of the students do not connect with the term *geography* and struggle, but obviously not Antoine.

Prompt: *Explain with examples what you mean when you write, "I am _____, the geographer."*

Key terms: *Alps, Andes, Berlin Wall, Cinder Cone, countries, dictators, extrusion, Germany, history, lava, Lava Cone, no solid rocks, museums, people and how lived, Russia, shield, three different types, volcanoes, World War II*

Expectations: 5–6 key terms; 6–7 sentences

I am Antoine, the geographer. I am writing about volcanoes and the three different types. The first one is the shield volcano. It is pretty much the lowest of all. The lava is so runny and there's no solid rocks in it. The second one is the Cinder Cone volcano. It is one of the tallest and steepest out of the three. It is the one you find the most of around the world. The Lava Cone is the third. It doesn't explode at all. It is a slow extrusion which mean expand. Then it hardens and makes a round mountain that looks like a bubble

—Antoine W, grade 7

ELA teachers (business, careers, literature, science, and social studies) often prompt students to respond to reading texts related to a course standard. A literature teacher modeled a Focused Free response to "Grace's Painful Pattern Repeated; Get It?" (www.readworks.org/passages/graces-painful-pattern-repeated-see-it).

Prompt: *What was the author's theme in the short story? Explain with examples from the text.*

Key terms: none provided, students were expected to use appropriate words and phrases from the text

Expectations: 6–7 key terms; 6–8 sentences

Actually, you might think that his passages has many themes as it refers to poetry, city streets, and even artwork as being a pattern. However, the underlying theme seems to focus on the development of a unique friendship with Grace and Pete as they coincidently discover and explore patterns in life. According to the text, Grace and Pete are discussing the meaning of sestina, a poetic pattern with stanzas in a interconnected configuration. This later lends Pete and Grace a new pattern of discussion . . . walking around the city. Later, Pete encounters a new friend with a new, a uncomfortable, pattern of contemporary art at the art gallery. At the end of the passage, the friendship of Grace and Pete becomes more evident through Pete's final words, "I attribute our new friendship to a rare state of grace."

— Marcetta W, academic coach

In response to the same prompt, Jana saw the theme of the story differently. It's always encouraging to see students follow a model without attempting to echo its content.

In the story "graces' Painful Pattern Repeated," the theme that stands out most is that life is a series of patterns. Pete's friend, Grace, said that the sestina was a old verse form of six stanzas that enamored her. When Pete didn't understand, she explained how the stanzas were connect by repeated phrases. Then she went on to complain that patterns in real life weren't that interesting. In fact they could get painfully boring. She had a pattern of walking on the same street to school every day. This caused Pete to consider patterns in his life, like taking the same bus every morning and afternoon. He remembered one afternoon an odd coincidence with a graceful girl named Sestina. He became enamored of her. They ended up getting off at the same us stop (who could have guessed?) and visiting a museum together. He preferred the paintings in the patterns of the old masters. She preferred contemporary art with patterns that Pete felt were painful. The story ended with Pete concluding that patterns, painful or not, were a part of life to be appreciated.

— Jana T, grade 9

Focused Free Writing Prompts and Course Standards

A progression for positioning Focused Free Writing increases students' depth and breadth of knowledge. In addition, it expands their awareness of the connection between what they write and what they already know from everyday life or have recently met in reading texts or class lessons.

Early Grades

Focused Free Writing within a Single Standard

It is easy to vary the Focused Free Writing prompts drawn on terms from within a standard.

Subject	Standard	Focused Free Writing prompts
ELA	Participate in collaborative conversations with diverse partners about *grade 2 topics and texts* with peers and adults in small and larger groups.	**Explain with examples your understanding of . . .** . . . listening, turn taking, gaining the floor or response to comments
Math	Know and apply the properties of integer exponents to generate equivalent numerical expressions. For example, $3^2 \times 3^{-5} = 3^{-3} = 1/3^3 = 1/27$.	. . . expressions, equations, square roots or perfect squares
Science	Students will describe various sources of energy and with their uses and conservation.	. . . the role of the sun, renewable energy or non-renewable energy
Social studies	The student will locate major topographical features.	. . . Prime Meridian, lines of latitude and longitude or the Mississippi River

Focused Free Writing across Standards or Subject Areas

When you begin including terms from more than one standard, the Focused Free Writing prompt helps students condition their thinking for later extended writing tasks. A Focused Free Writing prompt that contrasts and compare plants and animals is a good example.

Explain with Examples How Plants Differ from Animals

Plants are different from animals in lots of ways. Plants breathe in carbon dioxide and breath out oxygen. Animals breath in oxygen and breathe out carbon dioxide. Plants produce food like corn, broccoli and grain, and animals like cows and people eat them. The trunk or stem of plants hold their arteries and veins. A body or shell holds them for animals. I know about more differences, but that's all I have time for now.

— Sang-mi K, grade 4

No doubt this student is ready to construct an extended report on the major differences between organism in the plant and animals kingdoms. The same can be said for this older and more experienced writer.

How Mammals Differ from Crustaceans

There are an incredible number of ways that crustaceans are different from mammals. They are different in almost every way. I'll use people and shrimp to help you picture what I mean. The first thing you notice is the shrimp's external skeleton. People's skeletons are on the inside. This means that mammals don't have to molt as they grow, and their skeletons make them more agile than shrimp. Another thing is people live in small families and take years to raise their young. We learned in science that shrimp don't. The females lay thousands of eggs at a time and they leave the eggs to hatch and try to stay away from predators. Most shrimp don't. Crabs, starfish, puffins, dolphins, sharks and people prey on them or they would over-populate. That's called an ecosystem. That reminds me. People have communities and governments that protect them. Shrimp are on their own. I need more time to write about other differences.

— Renaldo H, grade 7

Interestingly, both students recalled much more to write than the 6 to 8 minutes in class permitted, and they seemed willing, even eager, to finish exploring and explaining the difference at a later time. Focused Free Writing seems to ignite new levels of curiosity.

Focused Free Writing Related to Everyday Life

Impressive insights show up in focused free writing when students relate new knowledge of course standards to events in everyday life that range from the mundane to surprising, even mysterious. One thing is certain. The connection that they have made to the standard solidifies the new knowledge in their minds for some time to come.

Benefits Teachers Attribute to the Use of Sentence Stems and Focused Free Writing

These two strategies have extraordinary impact on emerging writers (Sentence Stems) and independent writers (Focused Free Writing) as they construct their responses to new knowledge. They both guide the task of writing freely with

- lists of key terms,
- patterns of thought that students already possess within them,
- early structures that will develop later in their extended writing tasks (argument/opinion and informative/explanatory essays and narrative pieces), and
- sentences with standard capitalization and end punctuation.

They both build on students' tendency to write with a free association of the details of new knowledge with their own thought.

- The Sentence Stems strategy
    - builds on emerging writers' tendency to repeat sentence patterns that have worked for them in their earlier writing (*I love . . ., I like . . ., I have . . .*);
    - allows emerging writers to repeat a pattern indefinitely until they realize that it is no longer useful; and
    - serves as a jot list of writing topics for students to select and write more about at a later time.
    - "I thought Sentence Stems too repetitive at first, then the second time I used the strategy with my class, six of them started to replace the stem with other sentence patterns to include more details. The strategy really launched my students' growth in writing." (South Dakota public school teacher)
    - "I used to get upset with my first graders when they wrote *I like . . ., I like . . ., I like. . . .* Sentence stems has opened my eyes to how they actually promote and track students' development as writers." (North Carolina parochial school teacher)
    - "Most of my first graders moved beyond Sentence Stems after writing five entries. It was exciting to see that they moved beyond the safety of the repetition much sooner than I expected." (Mississippi special education teacher)
    - "Our students start with *I like . . .* stems and easily fill up a page of things they like. That page becomes a source of topics for writing later on free writing days. Students never ask, 'What should I write?' when they can write about anything they want. The list of sentence stems lasts all nine weeks." (Georgia curriculum director)
- The Focused Free Writing strategy
    - allows independent writers to use language patterns and style that they use most often,
    - shows students that free writing is much more than writing anything that comes to their minds, and
    - introduces jot lists of key terms in non-threatening writing tasks.
    - "I thought focused-free writing was only simple recall (DOK 1). Then the first time I used the strategy, six of my students showed unexpected

explanatory skills (DOK 2). They find focused free writing completely natural." (Georgia public school teacher)

- o "Before a system of constructed responses, students stayed engaged in free writing up until Halloween. Then it faded." (Illinois public school teacher)
- o "I used focused writing twice a week to help students interact with the extensive vocabulary of our rigorous religion curriculum. I've never seen so many students so comfortable writing and then talking about holy scripture." (Minnesota parochial school teacher)
- o "I've helped students keep current with their journal writing for my whole career. This is the first year that free writing hasn't become routine and uninteresting for students and for me." (South Carolina public school teacher)

- What students like about the Sentence Stems strategy:

  - o "We get to write the things we like."
  - o "We get to spell the best we can."
  - o "We can pick one to write about later."
  - o "We get to write as many [sentences] as we can."

- What students say about the Focused Free Writing strategy:

  - o "Free writing lets us write the way we are thinking."
  - o "It doesn't tell us how we are supposed to write."
  - o "I like the key words; they help me remember the important details for my writing."
  - o "The academic word list is best. I know I should use better vocabulary, but the easy words are the ones I think of. I just pick the academic word that means the same as the easy one I think of first."

Summing Up

The Sentence Stems and Focused Free Writing strategies are ideal to use early in students' progress of mastering the art and craft of constructed responses. They both prompt students to write the way they are already comfortable writing. Emerging writers write sentences that begin with the same stem of two or three words, *I like . . ., I have . . ., I promise. . . .* Independent writers write freely, following only the Five Key Practices as they respond to lessons or reading texts. As a result, they often start writing and run out of time to finish everything in their minds. This sets them up for further study and extended writing on topics about which they are curious and engaged. In early grades, students work from two vocabulary lists: sight words (used in all subject areas) and domain-specific words (used in specific ways in one subject area). Similarly, in the middle and upper grades, students meet and contribute to two vocabulary lists: words that are academic (appropriate for all subject areas; see Berkeley Unified SD Academic Vocabulary, http://www.nocread.com/busd/busd-grade-level-academic-vocabulary-berkeley-unified.html) and domain-specific words (used in specific ways or only in a subject area).

Suggested Readings

Lucy Calkins, *The Art of Teaching Writing*, 1970.
www.readworks.org/passages/graces-painful-pattern-repeated-see-it
Jean Piaget, *The Origins of Intelligence in Children*, 1952.

Chapter 6

Recalling Knowledge as Chunks in Writing

Chunking, in psychology, is a phenomenon whereby individuals group responses when performing a memory task. . . . [Individuals create] higher-order cognitive representations of the items on the list that are more easily remembered as a group than as individual items themselves. Representations of these groupings are highly subjective, as they depend critically on the individual's perception of the features of the items and the individual's semantic network.[1]

There has been much talk about mental chunking among educators for several decades, yet not many teachers nurture students in using the technique. The most obvious, simple example for Americans is the pattern of US phone numbers. All of us maintain a remarkable archive of phone numbers that we frequently call. We remember every 10-digit number important to us in chunks of

- area codes (three digits),
- exchange (three digits), and
- personal number (four digits).

Fortunately, mental chunking is just as simple and straightforward in writing. It is, however, not imposed from the outside like US telephone numbers; writers chunk their thoughts from the inside out. They remember chunks of language by pictures, which are much easier to recall than the words, phrases, and sentences that represent the pictures. The pictures give depth and richness to the words and help student writers pick just the right words because their readers need to see the pictures behind their words. Equally important for the writer: the pictures remain in their minds as they choose a constructed response to expand into an extended writing piece.

Framed Stories as Mental Chunking for Emerging Writers

The strategy for emerging writers called Framed Stories has evolved since the 1970s when it appeared as Framed Paragraphs in the Weehawken Integrated Language Arts (ILA) project.[2] ILA presented the strategy for independent writers in three steps.

- Select an informative passage extracted from current studies in your curriculum. For example, celebrations around the world led a teacher to select this passage celebrating a day in Mexico that made him curious, "Cinco de Mayo":

  Cinco de mayo is celebrated on the 5th of May. It does not celebrate Mexico's independence day from Spain like many believe. Rather, it remembers a David and Goliath-like fight. In 1862, the French invasion of Mexico began. Mexican General Ignacio Zaragoza's force of 4,000 soldiers defeated twice as many French soldiers in the Battle of Puebla.[3]

- Remove as much of the descriptive details (mental chunks or pictures) as possible while still leaving a frame of the structure of the paragraph.

  Cinco de mayo is celebrated _____. It does not celebrate Mexico's independence day _____. Rather, it remembers _____. In 1862, the French _____. Mexican General Ignacio Zaragoza's force of _____ defeated _____ French soldiers _____.

- Allow students 5 to 8 minutes to copy the framed paragraph and fill in details from the passage in their own words. Of course, there will be a huge variety of insertions, which is precisely the point of the framed paragraph. When student reconfigure new knowledge in their own words, they show ownership of the knowledge.

  Cinco de mayo is celebrated on the 5th of every May. It does not celebrate Mexico's independence day from the rule of Spain. Rather, it remembers a really lucky victory by the Mexican army. In 1862, the French started to take over the country of Mexico. Mexican General Ignacio Zaragoza's force of like 3000 troops surprised everybody and defeated like more than 6000 French soldiers near a little town.

  — Kin L, grade 6

Clearly, this reluctant middle school student shows control over what he has read, and we know that writing will extend his retention.

The same process of removing the mental chunks from passages works equally well with emerging writers. In a first grade study of seasons and weather early in the year, a male and female student had a different take on their summer weather experienced between kindergarten and first grade. Framed stories served to launch the year in writing quite efficiently.

The teacher designated a large bulletin board as a word wall for types of weather. He guided the students in brainstorming words that describe weather and human behavior related to weather. Types of weather from a science lesson included *rainy, snowy, sunny,* and *windy* days. Key words from the wall that the class of students identified as words related to sunny weather: *bikes, fishing, clear sky, outside, ride, short pants, sun, sunglasses, swimming, warm.*

Fun in the Sun

Everybody is ready to <u>drive a new car outside</u>. Let us put on sunglases and <u>drive a long time</u>. Outside in the sun, <u>we will kul down in a kul car</u>. I like sun because we <u>can drive anywar we want</u>. We can <u>come back anytim we want</u> and <u>nobody will aks about it</u>.

— Antoine, grade 1

Fun in the Sun

Everybody is ready to <u>have a grat time</u>. Let us put on a <u>parte in our bacyard</u>. Outside in the sun, <u>we will swim in are pul</u>. I like sun because we <u>don't have to come in erlee</u>. We can <u>pla chace</u> and lay owt.

— Kayla, grade 1

Obviously, students have an enormous archive of mental chunks of experiences in the summer sun. Two days later, the students completed a framed story titled, "Rainy Day." While the teacher planned other strategies for closing the lesson on windy weather, the students asked if they could write another framed story. Like so many other students, the strategy presented a certain attraction for these emerging writers.

Notice that the recall of information about sunny weather was positioned in the narrative genre of writing. Feel free to use the word *stories* in the title of the strategy loosely. The frame can easily provide a guiding structure for a short paragraph in the informational/explanatory and argument/opinion genres as the following student exemplars show.

Exemplars of Framed Stories Entries for and from Emerging Writers

For kindergarten, the frames begin with one or two sentences. They usually make familiar statements or start a story line.

Two little <u>robns</u> sitting on a <u>fens</u>.
Three little <u>chidrn</u> sitting on three <u>rocking chars</u>.
Four little <u>catrpillrs</u> sitting on a <u>big leef</u>.

— Demetrius, kindergarten

Students benefit from writing Framed Stories of all kinds. They can be simple narratives or patterns that follow a structure of a mode of informative/explanatory writing like cause-effect, compare-contrast, explain a process or problem-solution. Carletta and three PALs chose *How to drink milk at lunch.* They listed key words: *open, spread, wipe, napkin, lunchroom, sips.*

How to Drink Milk at Lunch

When I <u>open a carton of milk</u>, I <u>spread the top</u> first. Next I <u>spread the top open like a spout.</u> After that <u>I drink a little sips and wipe my mouth with a napkin.</u> That's how <u>I drink milk in our lunchroom.</u>

— Carletta, grade 1

Extending the Framed Stories Strategy to the Later Grades

While the Framed Stories strategy serves emerging writers as they move to the threshold of independent narrative writing, a good number of students ask for frames to use with all of their writing including extended essays. Multi-paragraph Framed Stories are called Framed Drafts. They serve independent writers as well as Framed Stories do emerging writers. These frames can introduce students to a number of modes of writing in informative/explanatory genres (such as character sketch, cause-effect, compare-contrast, explaining a process or problem-solution) and argument/opinion genres. See *A Writing Cycle for the Writing Process,*[4] for tested samples of Framed Drafts. Suffice it to say, Framed Stories or Framed Drafts have many uses that are only beginning to be discovered. Middle school teachers created these Framed Drafts in a summer workshop. Students were to add 2 to 5 words to each blank based on what they had recently read about pioneer, Daniel Boone:

> One of the first Americans to settle west of the mountains was Daniel Boone. He was born in _____ in _____. This was _____ after the birth of George Washington. When he was _____, his family moved _____. He became fond of _____. He excelled at _____ and _____, two very useful skills for pioneers.
>
> In _____, Boone and five others set out for Kentucky where they heard _____. For weeks they climbed _____ and _____. At last they came to _____ known as _____. After _____, the other men returned _____, but Boone _____. _____, _____, and _____ roamed there. It was _____ years before he return _____.

No doubt, the strategy can outlive its usefulness. Like the training wheels on a bicycle, many students are anxious about "keeping their balance" in their writing with the frames. So wean your students from the frames gradually, providing only 3 and then 2 sentences of the frame before moving them to the next level of scaffolding the development of mental chunking in the independent writing of students.

Copy and Continue for Independent Writers

The Copy and Continue strategy calls on mental chunking without the scaffold of a paragraph frame. You provide the main idea of a reading text or standards-based lesson for students to "copy." The opening sentence relieves students from the anxiety of how to start writing. The copied sentence launches them on their way to summarize the key points of the text or lesson in their own words. It moves the Framed Stories (or Framed Drafts) strategy to independent writing. Students rewrite content of a reading text or class lesson freely. A Copy and Continue prompt allows students to summarize a passage from a reading text or major part of a lesson

- without student's stretching to identify the main idea,
- in the same genre as it was presented,
- at the same level of DOK presented,
- while citing evidence from the source, and
- without focusing on writing skills more than writing content.

It goes without saying that when students put what they have been taught in their own words, it counts as evidence that they have learned it. The guidelines from the "Guide for Writing to Learn" goes like this:

1. Copy the part of the passage provided by your teacher for this entry.
2. Continue writing about the passage explaining fully the ideas that are in it.

The Copy and Continue strategy prompts students to recall key facts from a lesson or reading text with evidence from the source. As with all strategies for constructed response, the Five Key Practices apply. For the Copy and Continue strategy, the practices look like this.

	Key Practice	Description
I	Quantify your expectations for each constructed response.	Quantify the number of key terms and sentences you expect students to use in their response to every Copy and Continue entry that you prompt. • Note that the number of key terms are in addition to the word(s) used in the prompt (the opening sentence copied). • For grades 4–8 students, expect 5–6 key words from a word wall or brainstorm list. • Emphasize the need to refer to more than one part of a lesson or text.
2	Model your own response to Copy and Continue prompts the first couple of times.	Provide your model response to the prompt that you assigned to students. Make sure your model exceeds your expectations of student responses.

(Continued)

	Key Practice	Description
3	Guide student choices with a simple critical-thinking strategy.	All students read aloud the guidelines in the "Guide for Writing to Learn" for Strategy G. A choral reading assures that students are engaged in thought about the strategy. **Note:** Copy and Continue entries are written independently.
4	Prompt specific PALS strategies with each entry.	Using the response strategy that you assign, PALs complete the following sentence stem, "The strength of your writing is...." The source that students summarize determines the genre of the Copy and Continue entry.
5	Secure student self-assessment.	When students finish their entries, they complete the three-pronged self-assessment. 1. "I used key terms with meaning." 2. "I wrote meaningful facts." 3. "I used evidence from parts of the text or lesson." Students then read their entries aloud to their assigned PALs. PALs confirm (√) or question (?) each assessment.

When you prompt students to construct responses using the Copy and Continue strategy, present them with reading passages that are directly related to one or more standards of a course of study and require 5 to 6 thoroughly taught key terms in order to summarize the texts fully.

By the same token, students

- respond to the prompts more readily,
- find out what they understand about the a topic,
- write explanations that contribute to their classmates' understanding,
- learn from your model how to extract the main idea from whole passages,
- develop a critical-thinking habit to use the rest of their lives, and
- receive valuable practice in different genres of writing.

When students finish working with their PALs, ask if there is anyone who just heard their PAL read an entry that the rest of the class needs to hear. See if a PAL is identified who hasn't read aloud to the class in some time. As 2 or 3 PALs share their entry with the class, coach the class in responding with the PALS response strategy you have assigned.

There are other ways to position the Copy and Continue strategy. Consider the following techniques that have worked well for other teachers:

- Once students have completed 3 or 4 Copy and Continue entries that you prompt, set each group of 2 or 3 PALs up to review a passage relevant to your lesson. Give them 10 minutes to read the passage aloud among themselves and create a Copy and Continue prompt of their own. Circulate among the groups and select 2 or 3 exemplary ones to share with the class. Consider adding suitable ones to your archive of Copy and Continue prompts.

- As a follow-up task, provide a paired reading text for students to read and then insert additional details in their writing using evidence from that text.
- Allow some students to write with 2 PALs. One PAL copies the provided written passage. The second adds 1 or 2 sentences that describe the first related detail. The third adds a description of the second related detail. If there is an additional related detail, the first PAL adds a description of it.
- Project a number of passages from a unit of study on the interactive board. Let groups of 2 or 3 PALs select the one they want to respond using the Copy and Continue strategy.
- Prompt student writing as described above and quantify a number of academic terms that students need to include in their entries (see pp. 165, 170–171, 175).

Exemplars of Copy and Continue Entries for and from Teachers and Independent Student Writers

Early Grades

Calvin and his classmates listened to their teacher read a picture book aloud about a boy whose father returned home from a war with a battle wound. The teacher sensed a real engagement in the story, an empathy for the father. So she prompted them to respond with a text-to-self connection—*I have a battle wound on my arm*. Calvin sketched a picture of his wound on the back of his wrist and wrote,

> I have a battle wound on my arm.
> I was rib mi bike. [riding my bike]
> I was not hopn in the DiD. [hopping in the ditch]
> I Duw no like battle wons.
> It will go away and not come back.

—Calvin I, kindergarten

Later Grades

Gabriel finds that writing helps him wrap his mind around a topic. His Copy and Continue entry illustrates what he means. His list-writing style does show that he is pulling large chunks of new knowledge into about 10 sentences in a text-to-text connection.

Expectations: 5–6 key terms, 6–8 sentences

Key terms: *read, write, ability, jobs, standard of living, school attendence, economy, colonization, oppression*

> Illiteracy affects Africa in several ways . . . and the author of our textbook wrote about five of them, one being their ability to get a job. You need to be able to read and write to successfully maintain a job and move up. Another reason is the economies are really weak. It is so weak that the governments can't give anymore funds for education. The third reasons is the standard of living. Since most countries live in poverty education isn't that important; survival is. The fourth reason is that school attendence is low, which means not a lot of kids show up to school to get educated because they have to stay at home and work to support the family. The fifth reason is that ever since the colonization of Africa, all sorts of wars, funds and rules have been thrown around. This is a lot to overcome for a developing country when it is surrounded by countries just like it.
>
> — Gabriel J, grade 7

Copy and Continue Prompts and Course Standards

So far, the Copy and Continue prompts in this chapter focus on a single standard, unit, or course of study. Copy and Continue provides an obvious opportunity to ask students to provide a connection between two standards, units, or courses of study. At this level, students are moving out of summarizing a passage (DOK 1) and into inferring specific ideas about how separate lessons or texts relate (DOKs 2 through 4), depending on the extent to which they explain the connection.

When you begin including terms from more than one standard, the Copy and Continue prompt helps students condition their thinking for later extended writing tasks. To go on with the example of the plants and animals in the early grade, a prompt is as follows:

Copy . . .
   Although plants and animals are very different, they are alike in important ways.
   . . . and continue with the explanation from a text or class lesson.

Previous prompts on this topic focuses only on how plants and animals differ. Students' comfort levels with Copy and Continue help them enter the world of noting similarities where the differences are more pronounced. A good number of students surprise you with their insight. The task may require some students to work with PALs. An example of an entry written by young PALs reads like this (4–5 key terms, 5–6 sentences).

Although plants and animals are very different, they are alike in important ways. The writer says they both need food and water. Some animals eat plants, some eat animals, and some eat both plants and animals. Plants have roots that get nutrients from the soil. Second, they reproduce. Animals have babies and plants make new plants with seeds. And we use plants to make baskets or furniture like tables and chairs. We use animals to make clothes and make food like cheese. Animals and plants are way more alike than people think.

— Aaron and Mykisha, grade 3[5]

Aaron wrote the first and third parts of the entry. Mykisha wrote the second and fourth. They wrote the final sentence together.

An older student demonstrated how he responded to the difference between two classes of animals. His Copy and Continue prompt required him to go to another source for evidence, although it is likely some of his details are his own.

Copy . . .

Our textbook describes how classes of animals are different. That is why they are in different classes. Yet the similarities between mammals and birds are impossible to overlook.

. . . and continue with the explanation from an outside text and your observations.

Actually, there are more similarities than I can include in 10 minutes. One author wrote they are both warm-blooded vertebrates. They have body systems and care for their young. Since both are warm-blooded, they don't rely on "external heart sources." This makes it possible for them to live anywhere there is land. They both have internal bone structures although birds bones are mostly light and hollow so they can fly. They both have digestive, circulatory and nervous systems, too. Most important, they both care for their young. Make sure, the care is very different among birds and among mammals. Birds like geese mate for life and care for goslings until they fly away to try life on their own. Other birds like robins, push their babies out of the nest and wish them well within weeks. Birds do not recognize their parents after they are independent. Mammals can hang together for generations, but that's getting into differences. There is really more to learn about animals than there is time in life.

— Dai Foo, grade 10[6]

Benefits Teachers Attribute to the Use of Framed Stories and Copy and Continue

These two strategies impact emerging writers (Framed Stories) and independent writers (Copy and Continue) in two ways since both strategies

1. Confront them directly with writing about new knowledge. The strategies almost guarantee that the writers respond to the prompt in a logical fashion.
2. Provide a scaffold or launch that guides them through the details.

Additionally, both strategies can be altered for use by both emerging and independent writers. Framed Stories can expand from a paragraph-long narrative frame to a multi-paragraph essay frame. Copy and Continue prompts can be reduced from 2 or 3 sentences to a single or even part of a sentence for emerging writers. Primary teachers have called these sentence-parts "story starters"; they can be positioned to start students' ideas in all three core writing genres.

- The Framed Stories strategy

  o reduces anxiety about sentence structure with marginal writers,
  o enhances sentence variety among all writers,
  o insures that every sentence begins with a capital letter and ends with appropriate punctuation,
  o allows students to focus on the message in their thoughts, and
  o provides intensive practice with the revision strategy of sentence expansion.

    - "I thought Framed Stories too formulaic, that is, until my students used one for the first time. The frames actually entranced them, and they became competitive, adding the most surprising word pictures to their writing I had ever seen." (South Dakota public school teacher)
    - "I'm surprised. I thought my students' writing would all be alike. Not true! The frame doesn't restrict my first graders' thoughts. It does just the opposite. Frames prompt greater variety than any other strategy I'm using." (Tennessee parochial school teacher)
    - "Framed stories is another strategy Dr. Combs has re-invented with remarkable positive impact on student writing. I'm learning to expect him to find a marginal strategy and figure out a way to unleash its potential." (Georgia State ELA Consultant)
    - "They copy the frame and add words like they are playing *Mad Libs*. No, better than *Mad Libs*; they get really silly with that game. Framed stories keep their thoughts on a productive focus." (Tennessee parochial school teacher)
    - "Where has this strategy been for my twenty-year career in teaching? I've never seen a strategy free students' minds to be creative with expanding ideas." (South Carolina public school teacher)

- "For years I told teachers to avoid frames in writing. I wish I could take that advice back. Now the Framed Stories strategy is my go-to strategy to demonstrate with kindergartners writing at pattern 6 and above (p. 47)." (Georgia curriculum director)

- The Copy and Continue strategy

  - allows independent writers to use language patterns and style that they use most often,
  - shows students that free writing is much more than writing anything that comes to their minds,
  - introduces jot lists of key terms in non-threatening writing tasks, and
  - shows them that academic vocabulary is as important as domain-specific vocabulary.

    - "What a simple solution to all students I meet who struggle with identifying the main idea in a reading text. After I reword the main idea in a Copy and Continue prompt 4–5 times, they catch right on." (South Carolina public school teacher)
    - "Last month, I used Copy and Continue five times with my fourth graders. Each time I included less and less of the main idea. And you know what, my students didn't even notice they were starting to identify main ideas themselves." (Minnesota parochial school teacher)
    - "Copy and Continue was the perfect strategy for formative assessment in the prehistory unit of the History of the Americas. I could see that some of my less attentive students were understanding this foundational unit." (Georgia high school US history teacher)
    - "For years, I thought the elementary teachers weren't teaching students the concept of main idea-supporting details. The first time I used Copy and Continue, three of my students asked, 'So you want us to start our constructed responses with the main idea?'" (Georgia social studies teacher)

- What students say about the Framed Stories strategy:

  - "Framed stories are easy and fun."
  - "This is my longest story ever!"
  - "I love reading my stories to my mom."
  - "I added the most words to the frame today, and I wasn't even trying."
  - "We can add as many words as we want."

- What students say about the Copy and Continue strategy:

  - "I used to have trouble getting started in writing. C & C helps a lot."
  - "Ms. Jimenez is the first teacher who showed me how to start a constructed response. I've got it now."

- o "When I know the first sentence, I understand what I'm supposed to write."
- o "Copy and Continue helps me remember what I've read, especially in Physical Science class."
- o "I can see exactly what I'm learning when I write the lesson in my own words."

Summing Up

The Framed Stories and Copy and Continue strategies follow the Sentence Stems and Focused Free Writing strategies nicely. They provide more structure for students and move them towards writing in traditional modes of the three core writing genres. Framed Stories actually provide the format of the writing in its entirety. Copy and Continue presents just the main idea but sets students up to write an entry in the same genre as the text or part of a lesson that they are summarizing. Both strategies serve as prompts that consistently move students into depths of knowledge (DOKs 2 and 3) that exceed simple recall (DOK 1).

Notes

1. https://en.wikipedia.org/wiki/Chunking_(psychology)
2. Weehawken Board of Education, *Individualized Language Arts: Diagnosis, Prescription, Evaluation*, 1973.
3. Full passage, www.apples4theteacher.com/holidays/cinco-de-mayo/about.html
4. Warren E. Combs, *A Writing Cycle for the Writing Process*, 2013, pp. D-10–D-32.
5. Student response based on www.ehow.com/how-does_5438233_animals-plants-similar.html
6. www.ehow.com/info_8439713_similarities-between-birds-mammals.html

Chapter 7

Sharpening Understanding of Closely Related Words
(Phrases, Numbers, Symbols, or Formulas)

One of these is not like the others, I heard my 3-year old daughter sing these words over and over again, tirelessly in a monotone except for the word *not.* She swirled a pile of colorful buttons on the floor in front of her with one hand and fished one out to hold over her head, *Here's one.* Once she set the different one aside, I heard the eight-word tune once again—again and again—until it stopped to the high-pitched squeal, *Here's another one.*

I have seen pre-K and kindergarten teachers show flashcards with four figures on them like 2, 4, 7, and W. One teacher presented four flashcards grouped together in the same arrangement. The task? Explain why one of these is different from the others.

	2	4
	W	7

Of course, this is an age-old childhood past time that springs directly from the mental reactions of infants to the appearance of novel objects or characters in their line of sight.

- Tall people with facial hair over there, other tall people closer, people my size up close, reach for all furry animals

The first time facial hair shows up, the reaction may include a convincing display of tears. Later, it is an important game that rolls out with deliberation.

- Blue buttons in one group, red buttons in a second, yellow in a third
- Tall people with facial hair over there, other tall people closer, people my size up close, chase all furry animals

Interestingly, categorizing new living things, objects, events, and places continues to serve children well into adolescence and the rest of their lives. As they meet new and diverse experiences, they try placing these experiences into existing categories that help them make sense of them for ourselves. When they run into new knowledge that does not fit a category, they create a new framework of categories. An important job for us as their teachers is to help students set up new categories for all of the new knowledge and experiences they will meet that don't fit in any of their existing categories. Noticing what parts of new experiences are different and alike is as important to their growth and well-being as maintaining sufficient access to food and shelter.

Consequently, noticing and explaining similarities and differences offers a role to constructed responses for learning. It's the perfect strategy for moving students beyond the simple recall of DOK 1 to conceptualizing new knowledge in helpful ways. Like so many growth opportunities in life, we can prompt students in hard or easy ways:

- We can tell them that we are going to help them become deeper thinkers, talking on and on about DOK 1 and DOK 2 and how important the mental habits of DOK 2 are for them to acquire. We can talk at length about the several strategies of an author's or our craft in presenting meaning in reading texts or class lessons.
- Or, we can invite them to play the *Sesame Street* song[1] and watch students discover the author's or your craft with a strategy that they have used since well before they could talk or walk.

I call it the Quad Cluster strategy, and the guide is as follows:

1. Write the four terms (phrases, numbers, symbols, or formulas) at the top of the page.
2. Circle the one that is different from the other three, "One of these things is not like the others."
3. Write 2 or 3 sentences about how the circled word is different.
4. Write 2 or 3 more sentences about how the other three are alike.

Quad Clusters for Emerging Writers

With students in grades K-1 or older Special Ed, ESOL, or EL students, introduce the cluster of four on chart paper or an interactive board. Download the tune, "One of these things is not like the others," from the Internet and follow the lead of the creators of *Sesame Street*.

- Place the four words, symbols, or numbers in plain view

    red   seven
    yellow   green

    and sing the *Sesame Street* song. By the time you have completed the second verse aloud with your students, several of them have their hands in the air, waving them and saying, "I know! I know! I've got it!"

- And indeed some of them do. When you and they reach consensus that the different word is "seven," the fun has just begun. The Quad Cluster strategy is not about guessing the "right" answer but rather explaining why one choice is, in fact, the different one that leaves the other three alike.
- It is time to let the students explain why "seven" is the different word in this Quad Cluster. Let one student at a time coach you through what to write for them on the chart.

  - Juan may start, "Seven is the different word." You write the 5-word sentence just as he speaks it and place his name in parentheses after the word "word."
  - Lakisha chimes in with, "It is a number like one or two."

- You may conclude that the class has explained how "seven" is different. Now it's time to explain how that other three are alike.

  - Ahim starts, "Red, yellow and green are colors."
  - Susan, "Red is a color on stop signs."
  - Carl, "The sun is the color yellow."
  - "My mom goes when the light is green," concludes Nuri.

- You post the entry of 6 sentences along with each student's name on the wall for all to see for a week or so and let the students "read" their sentences for classmates and visitors to their class.

Red, Seven, Yellow, Green

Seven is the different word (Juan).
It is a number like one or two (Lakisha).
Red, yellow and green are colors (Ahim).
Red is the color on stop signs (Susan).
The sun is really bright yellow so don't look at it (Carl).
My mom goes fast when the light is green (Nuri).

- Challenge some of your more confident readers and writers to recall or even read several of the sentences from the top.
- Continue letting group of 6 students dictate the sentences of a Quad Cluster entry for you to write and place on the wall for them to "read" to others throughout a week or two.

Eventually, emerging writers will tell you when they are ready to start constructed responses to lessons or texts with the Quad Cluster strategy completely on their own. Here are several entries written by kindergarten and first grade students in the spring of their school year.

Exemplars of Quad Cluster Entries from Emerging Writers

As a review, Kayla's class listed the key words needed to explain the two different math operations they experienced so far.

Prompt: *sum, plus, difference, addend*

Key terms: *add, answer, difference, minus, plus, subtract, sum*

Difference is different. It is a answer for subtract. Sum and plus and addend are for adding. That is all.

— Kayla, grade 1

After a study of family life, kindergartners were introduced to the Quad Cluster on chart paper. On the third cluster, Quantavious insisted that he write his own on his own paper. As you already know, his teacher complied.

Prompt: *sister, mother, cousin, brother*

Key terms: *family, house, together, eat, sleep, work, study*

Cousin is the different word. Sister and mother and brother all live in the same <u>house</u>. They <u>eat</u> and <u>sleep</u> in the house. My cousins does not.

— Quantavious, kindergarten

Quad Clusters for Independent Writers

The Quad Cluster strategy for emerging writers is all about singing the song and playing the Quad Cluster game. Especially as students develop the habit of contributing to each small-group entry, they offer remarkable insight in explaining why one word doesn't belong. They don't hold back and capture the essential relationship among the terms. For example, Ahim reads the following Quad Cluster:

rose, tulip, oak, daisy

He declares, "*Oak* is a tree and the other three are flowers," and you can support his claim by asking, "So these are two types of plants. Is that what you are saying?" As Ahim agrees, you can announce. So *oak* is one class of plant and *rose, tulip,* and *daisy* belong to another class of plants. The relationship between one term to three terms is critical to understanding and probing the power inherent in using the Quad Cluster strategy.

With independent writers, the procedure for presenting constructed responses changes. Like all previous critical-thinking strategies, the Quad Cluster reaches its full power with the support of the Five Key Practices. See the list of seven basic relationships of Quad Cluster and Analogy prompts on page 90.

	Key Practice	Description
1	Quantify your expectations for each constructed response.	Quantify the number of key terms and sentences you expect students to use in their response to every Quad Cluster you prompt. • Note that the number of key terms are additional key terms students used to explain the relationship of the 4 terms in the prompt, not the 4 terms themselves. • Expect 4–6 sentences. Expecting fewer sentences encourages students to construct responses that show less of what they know.
2	Write your own personal response to Quad Cluster prompts the first couple of times.	Provide your model response to the prompt that you assigned to students. Even if they echo your model, they are practicing a response that follows the "Guide for Writing to Learn" (see eResources). The structure of your response to the cluster is novel to them, and attempting to parrot what they heard you read accelerates their awareness and mastery of the strategy. Make sure your model exceeds your expectations of student responses.
3	Guide student choices with a simple critical-thinking strategy.	All students read aloud the guidelines in the "Guide for Writing to Learn" for Strategy E. A choral reading of the four guidelines documents that students are engaged in thought about the strategy.
4	Prompt specific PALS strategies with each entry.	Using only the strategy you assign, PALs complete the following Sentence Stem, "The strength of your writing is...." Most often the informational genre fits a Quad Cluster entry, although there a times when an open cluster (one with more than one logical choice) leads to a well-defined argument.
5	Secure student self-assessment.	When students finish their entries, they complete the three-pronged self-assessment. 1. "I used key terms with meaning." 2. "I wrote meaningful sentences." 3. "I used evidence from parts of the text or lesson." Students then read their entries aloud to their PALs and show in their writing evidence of the three scores. PALs agree (√) or question (?) each score.

When you prompt students to construct responses to Quad Clusters, serve them terms, numbers, phrases, symbols, equations, or formulas around seven basic relationships common in our understanding of the world around us.

Target Quad Clusters

No.	Relationship	Quad Cluster
1	Part-to-whole	ratio, fraction, proportion, **whole number***
2a	Antonym	cold, frigid, freezing, **scorching***
2b	Synonym	soaking, sopping, dripping, **wet***
3	Cause-effect	state's rights, slavery, territorial expansion, **US Civil War***
4	Member-class	vassal, serf, lord, **fiefdom***
5	Class-class	dividend, quotient, **product**,* divisor
6	Problem-solution	l, w, h, **V***
7	Definition (or example)	sweet-spirited, beautiful, hard-working, **Cinderella***

Let me guess. When you read the example for Relationship 2, synonyms—*soaking, sopping, dripping, wet**—you thought, "Wait just a minute." These are all alike, four synonyms that mean *wet*! Exactly, however, *soaking, sopping,* and *dripping* are three members of the class of *wet*. And so are *clammy, damp, humid,* and *moist*. *Wet* is one enormous and, therefore, important class to children and adults for categorizing and defining experiences. Other word classes of synonyms include *hot, cold, light,* and *precipitation*. They each have a wide range of related words each with a wide variety of important nuances within them.

The relationships in the above table are constant, so teachers refer to these clusters as "target" Quad Clusters. There is arguably one logical choice that leaves three other choices that are very much alike.

When all of your Quad Cluster prompts highlight one of these several relationships, you

- Create clusters more readily,
- Harvest more of the power of the cluster, and
- Help students recast the vocabulary of new knowledge in an increasing number of ways.

By the same token, students

- Find them easier to analyze and interpret,
- Write explanations that are more likely to stay with them,
- Develop a critical-thinking habit to use the rest of their lives, and
- Fine-tune their innate drive to categorize parts of the world around them.

These benefits among your students appear as increased precise vocabulary in class discussions and written class reports. Their performance on tests of knowledge in your subject area rises significantly because they have significant, improved control over the language of the content area.

So as you look for ways of employing the Quad Cluster strategy for activating or summarizing key concepts in learning, consider the following progression of constructed responses to Quad Cluster prompts with your students:

- Begin with target clusters that mark the term "not like the others" with an asterisk in the prompt. When you position the first part-to-whole cluster, see if some of your students can identify the relationship. There's a good chance one or more of your students will.

*dividend, divisor, quotient, **division****

Division is the different word, the "whole," the name of a math operation. *Dividend, divisor,* and *quotient* are three essential features. Continue to serve up target clusters until you are certain students understand that Quad Clusters are not about get the "right" answer, but rather being able to explain why the targeted term is a logical choice.

After 3 to 5 clusters with a marked term, drop the asterisk and let students identify the different term in small-groups, with an assigned PAL, and eventually on their own.

- "Open" Quad Clusters make up the second step of the progression. Present prompts that require students to select the item that they see as not like the others.

cat, catfish, whale, wolf

In this cluster, students logically support two choices; both signal a class-to-class relationship.

*cat, **catfish**,* whale, wolf*

three mammals and one fish [actinopterygii by secondary students]

*cat, catfish, whale, **wolf****

three domesticated and one untamed/wild animal

Actually, your students will help you discover open clusters. When you serve up what you think as a target cluster without an asterisk, some students select a term that is different from your intended choice and support it with insightful logic. Here is an example of such a cluster:

cat, catfish, whale, woman

A middle school teacher of life science discovered this on one of my visits to his class. In the first class of the day, one or more students circled each of the four and supported their choices with solid reasons. Of course, *catfish* was the choice the teacher intended since the choice aligns with standard on which the lesson was based. Yet at least one student justified each of the other three.

- *woman* (higher-order thinker, the only gender-specific term, verbal language user; tool user)
- *whale* (mobility and agility; whales eat everything that gets in the way of their open mouths; agile does not describe them; the other three have distinguishing palates and move about quickly)
- *cat* (averse to water; they drink water, but don't get into it; they give themselves tongue baths; the other three are very comfortable submerged or partially submerged in water.)

The teacher aptly brought closure to the discussion of this open cluster. Instead of glibly concluding that there is no right answer in Quad Clusters (which is not the case), he simply said, "You used logic in defending each of your choices; however, when you see a choice like this on an end-of-grade test, you better choose *catfish*. Someone explain why."

- Conclude with student-created clusters, ones created by students based on a core standard in a course of study. The caveat here is that one of the seven relationships may not be included even though the outlier is definitely not like the other three and the other three are alike. When students bring clusters to class, give the class no more than 20 to 30 seconds to identify and defend a logical choice. Check out this example from Cory, a middle school history student who offered this cluster in a unit on colonial America. Note how he blended a key term of a standard (*Society of Friends*) into his prior knowledge of the world around him. To date, no group of students or teachers has selected the intended term in fewer than 30 seconds.

diamond, dog, emerald, Society of Friends

Society of Friends seems to be the distraction. Students often say, "*Society of Friends* because we studied it." or "*Society of Friends* because it is three words and capital letters." Cory responds to either of these with, "Please people. Think!" Then he explains that all terms describe things that people value highly. *Society of Friends* is not a logical choice; the capital letters and inclusion of three words are ruses. It is *emerald* that is not like the others since all of the other terms have strong connections to friendship. *Diamond* is a woman's best friend; a *dog* is man's best friend, and the *Society of Friends* describes the friendship of fellow Christians. Quakers believed that their meeting houses highlighted the most important friendship they experience on earth.

Field trips or common experiences are perfect opportunities for students to uncover Quad Clusters for themselves. Teachers have asked students to identify three terms that are alike and one that is different based on their recent restaurant experience for the evening.

- *Thickburger, Whopper, Double Stack,* **hamburger** (member-to-class)
- **napkin**, *fork, knife, spoon* (class-to-class)
- *greeter, wait person, cook,* **diner** (class-to-class)
- *tasty, juicy, filling,* **entree** (definition)
- *fried chicken, T-bone steak, pork chop,* **chocolate pie** (class-to-class)

Participants at one of our Coaches Model Classroom workshops for building leaders take the same restaurant task to the next level.

- *attentive server, tasty food, ironed table cloths,* **repeat** *customer* (three causes to one effect)
- **well-run business**, *full parking lot, regular customers, community involvement* (one cause to three effects)
- *horse-radish crusted salmon,* **fried green tomatoes**, *lamb in parchment, praline chicken* (class-to-class: courses of meal)

Younger students see that Quad Cluster is an obvious invitation to spontaneous play. They serve up clusters in an effort to stump their friends, a parent, or teacher. A second grader prompted

- *sister, grandma, aunt, brother* (class-to-class relationship of gender)

Yes, it is *brother,* the only male. A classmate followed with

- *brother, mother, sister, cousin* (class-to-class relationship of generation)

Older students can give into the lure of Quad Cluster play, too.

- *10 mph grace,* **left turn on red**, *complete stops only, right turn on red* (class-to-class: legal vs. illegal driving procedure)
- *no license, no insurance card, no seatbelt,* **no passenger** (class-to class; legal vs. illegal)

It's interesting that in this game, the relationship implied in the first prompt is often the one that guides several successive one. The game is usually over when the prompts become illogical, random, inappropriate, or just plain silly.

It is fine for Quad Clusters to morph to the level of entertainment, even go viral like *Mad Libs*; however, in class, written responses to Quad Cluster prompts stored in a class learning log (or journal) is absolutely critical. It is when the prompting and writing of Quad Cluster responses follow the Five Key Practices (p. 89) that students receive the full benefit of this powerful critical-thinking strategy.

Exemplars of Quad Cluster Entries for and from Independent Writers

Early Grades

Students will investigate the characteristics and basic needs of plants and animals. Human needs are included in the study of basic needs of animals.

Prompt: *mother, cousin, brother, sister*

Key terms: *animal, aunt, basic need, child, cousin, family, female, grandparent, male, parent, related, uncle, brother, sister, mother*

Teacher model (written and read to students prior to their first quad cluster):

Cousin is the different word in this cluster. Mother, brother and sister make up a <u>family</u>. Family is a <u>basic need</u> of humans and some other animals. Mother is one of the parents, and brother and sister are <u>children</u> of the parents. A cousin is part of another <u>related</u> family. A cousin can be a girl or a boy. Brothers are <u>male</u>; girls and mothers are <u>female</u>.

Student exemplar that exceeds expectations:

Cousin is the different word, no, mother is. I'm a cousin and Bella and Avery and Rylan are sisters. Mother is a <u>parent</u>. Brother and sister and cousin are all a <u>child</u>. My mama and <u>Auntie</u> Erin are sisters, and <u>Uncle</u> Taylor is a brother.

— Timothy, grade 1

Notice how Timothy starts to emulate his teacher's model entry, but it does not take him more than four words (a good while in the handwriting of first graders) to change his mind. Then, he explains the paradigm in his mind. Contrary to the lesson presentation of the nuclear family that does not include the cousin, he sees a stronger pattern of generation in the cluster.

Later Grades

Special needs student Vanessa loves Quad Clusters. Her teacher is quite pleased. Vanessa studies hard and often gets most of her new facts almost right. Her response is typical, and she looks forward to a sticky note 60-second conference with her teacher to fine-tune her understanding.

Prompt: *Germany, England, Ukraine, Russia*

Expectations: 5–6 key terms; 6–8 sentences

Key terms: *communist, eastern block, democracy, parliamentary, presidential, economies, command, market, blended, standard of living, private enterprise, state-owned factories*

England is not like Germany, Ukraine and Russia because the other three are communists countries. England is a presidential democray. It has a market economy and high standard of living than the other three.

Ukraine, Russia and Germany are alike because they are communist countries. Not only that, they have command economies where the state owns lots of the factories. Not only that, these countries are against democracy. Ukraine is in Russia and Germany fought along with Russia in World War I.

A list on a sticky note was signed with a smiley face.

1. England = parliamentary
2. East German WAS communist, not now
3. Ukraine WAS in Russia, not now
4. Germany and Russia fought AGAINST, not with

Quad Clusters and Course Standards

A second progression for positioning Quad Clusters serves to increases students' depth and breadth of knowledge. In addition, it expands their awareness of connection between what they write and what they already know from everyday life or have recently met in reading texts or class lessons.

Early Grades

Clusters within a Single Standard

It is easy to vary the Quad Clusters drawn on terms from within a standard using the seven relationships.

Current standard from Life Science: Understand how to investigate the characteristics and basic needs of plants and animals

- *stem, **bush**, leaf, root* (part-to-whole)
- *energy, **growth**, living space, food* (cause-to-effect)
- *lion, hippopotamus, giraffe, **kitten*** (class-to-class: wild to domestic)

Clusters across Standards

When you begin including terms from more than one standard, the relationships can become more interesting. They go beyond the seven relationships presented earlier.

Current standard from Life Science: Understand how to investigate the characteristics and basic needs of plants and animals

Previous standard from Earth Science: How to observe, measure, and communicate weather data to see patterns in weather and climate

- o *stem,* **mercury,** *leaf, root* (class-to-class: three parts of a plant to one part of a thermometer)
- o *stem,* **rain,** *leaf, root* (members of a class vs. one basic need of plants)
- o *energy,* **growth,** *living space, food* (cause-to-effect)

Clusters Related to Everyday Life

The interesting relationships among terms continue to unfold when you include terms from everyday life. Inserting everyday terms into Quad Clusters ensures that students store new knowledge in among structures of prior knowledge. Neuroscience research suggests that new knowledge tied to prior knowledge does not wash away from students' minds during the next night's sleep.

Current standard from Life Science: Understand how to investigate the characteristics and basic needs of plants and animals

Everyday life of the writer at home: Awareness of characteristics and basic needs of students in family life.

- o *stem,* **feet,** *leaf, root* (class-to-class: three parts of a plant to one part of the human body)
- o *sunlight, rose, carbon dioxide,* **8-hours sleep** (two causes of healthy growth in a plant; one cause of healthy growth in the student writer)
- o *energy,* **growth,** *living space, food* (cause-to-effect)

Middle Years
Clusters within a Single Standard

Middle grades standards are more complex; one standard may consist of several distinct elements. It is easy to vary the Quad Clusters drawn on terms from within a standard using the seven relationships.

Current standard from math: Identify parts of an expression using mathematical terms (sum, term, product, factor, quotient, coefficient); view one or more parts of an expression as a single entity.

- *factor, collect like terms, distribute, **linear expression*** (definition)
- *factor, **expression**, term, coefficient* (part-to-whole)
- *taiga, rainforest, desert, **plateau*** (class-to-class: biome to landform)

Clusters across Standards

The relationships among words across standards or different elements of a standard become increasingly interesting. These two elements show how.

Current standard from math: Identify parts of an expression using mathematical terms (sum, term, product, factor, quotient, coefficient); view one or more parts of an expression as a single entity.

Previous standard from math: Write expressions that record operations with numbers and with letters standing for numbers.

- $2 (8 + 7), 2 (7 + 8), 8 (2 + y), (7 + 8) 2$ (three equivalent expressions; one unequal expression)
- $5 (7) + 5 (3), 5 (7 + 3), 5 (3 + 7), 5 (y + 7)$ (synonyms: four equivalent expressions)

Clusters Related to Everyday Life

Terms from everyday life can fit into these middle grade math clusters, and they help students connect new knowledge about expressions solidly in their brains.

Current standard from middle grade math: Understand how to investigate the characteristics and basic needs of plants and animals

Everyday life of the writer at home: Awareness of characteristics and basic needs of students in family life.

- *number, **left fielder**, letter, term* (class-to-class: three parts of an expression to one part I play on our baseball team)
- *bicycle, family car, my classroom, **expression*** (three things with parts I experience daily; one math entity with parts)

Later Grades

Clusters within a Single Standard

It is easy to vary the Quad Clusters drawn on terms from within a standard using the seven relationships.

Current standard from World History: Analyze the relationship among Christianity, Judaism, and Islam.

- *Christianity, **monotheism**, Judaism, Islam* (member-to-class)
- *Christianity, **Abraham**, Islam, Judaism* (cause-to-effect)
- *monotheistic, Torah, Southwest Asia, **Judaism*** (definition)

Clusters across Standards

Since success in college and career is the goal of teaching and learning, prompting students to write across standards in the later grades is absolutely essential. Feel free to ask students to write across standards that they meet within a window of a month or two. The teaching of the following two standards is two months (and several centuries) apart.

Current standard from World History: Analyze the relationship among Christianity, Judaism, and Islam.

Previous standard from World History: Explain the development and impact of Hinduism and Buddhism on India and subsequent diffusion of Buddhism.

- ***Hinduism**, Christianity, Islam, Judaism* (class-to-class: three monotheistic and one polytheistic religion)
- ***Quran**, Buddhism, Hinduism, Confucianism* (class-to-class: one holy text to three religions with a holy text)
- *systematic theology, deity, **freedom of belief**, holy text* (class-to-class: religious authority to political right)

Clusters Related to Everyday Life

The interesting relationships among terms continue to unfold when you include terms from everyday life. Inserting everyday terms into Quad Clusters ensures that students store new knowledge in among structures of prior knowledge. Neuroscience research suggests that new knowledge tied to prior knowledge does not wash away from students' minds during the next night's sleep.

Current standard from World History: Analyze the relationship among Christianity, Judaism and Islam.

Everyday life of the writer as a US citizen: Practice of the freedom of religion and other freedoms guaranteed by the *US Constitution*.

- *moral code, **freedom of religion**, central authority, sacred text* (class-to-class: three features of a monotheistic religion to one feature of the bill of rights of the *US Constitution*)
- *freedom of the press, freedom of speech, pursuit of happiness, **code of morality*** (class-to-class: three guarantees of a democratic society, one feature of a religious tradition)

Benefits Teachers Attribute to the Use of Quad Clusters

It is clear that the Quad Cluster strategy has extraordinary power in developing student mastery of constructed responses for learning.

- Huge vocabulary building:

  - "My first child refused to write about any new knowledge in our home-school curriculum. It was Quad Clusters that enabled him to write his first response to a geography unit, and he has never looked back." (North Dakota home-school parent of six)
  - "I've never had so many students use the language of math in class discussions until I prompted a Quad Cluster each week." (South Dakota public school teacher)
  - "The Quad Cluster has shifted my class into high gear. Over 2/3 of my students are highly engaged in class and small-group discussions." (Tennessee parochial school teacher)
  - "Quad Cluster doesn't teach math, but it is making my students talk like mathematicians. Our 4th graders set a school record with 91 percent meeting and 64 exceeding state standard on a criterion-referenced test." (Georgia public school principal)
  - "Quad Clusters have helped me the degree that my first-grade son understands the vocabulary in our lessons. Knowing this allows me to help him overcome the limits of his perceptions." (North Carolina home-school parent)

- A favorite strategy of students:

  - A parent reported that elementary school students play the Quad Cluster game in the back seat of the car on way home from school.
  - A teacher reported students bringing unsolicited Quad Clusters to school for his class to try out.

- Follows the routine of creating and responding to selected-response strategies.

  - Terms of the Quad Clusters derive from the vocabulary of standards-based lessons.
  - Analyzing four choices and finding a logical reason for choosing one mirrors the process of solving selected-response test items.

- Builds on the innate propensity of children to classify the features of the world around them.
- Is a sure way to vault students' minds into higher-order thinking in a matter of minutes.

Summing Up

From the length of this chapter, it is obvious that teachers at all grade levels call on the Quad Cluster with great frequency. It is simple for the youngest of writers yet inoffensive for the most advanced. More than any other strategy, it expands students' working vocabulary. Students acquire new vocabulary (including words, equations, phrases, numbers, symbols, and formulas) from two distinctive lists: 1) subject-specific or domain-specific words (used only in a subject area) and 2) words that are recognized only by sight for emerging writers and or academic (words used in any subject area). It helps students fine-tune their understanding of closely related words, equations, phrases, numbers, symbols, or formulas. It advances word study into a world of relationships among words. It accomplishes all of this in a completely painless way, almost like singing a song that won't leave your mind. And thanks to this strategy for preparing your students for the rigors of the next chapter, one that focuses as much on the relationship of words, equations, phrases, numbers, symbols, and formulas as it does the meaning of each itself.

Note

1. *Sesame Street,* "One of These Things Is Not Like the Other," www.metrolyrics. com/one-of-these-things-is-not-like-the-others-lyrics-sesame-street.html; *Sesame Street,* "Three of These Things Belong Together," https://www. youtube.com/watch?v=2VFG5fQHMro

Chapter 8

Arriving in a World of Analogies

(Words, Equations, Phrases, Ideas, Events, Numbers, Symbols, or Formulas)

Roses are red
Violets are blue
Sugar is sweet
And so are you!

My first batch of home-made valentines for the classmates at school included this children's rhyme that I sent to Mary Jane McDonald in second grade. All I, like any other red-blooded boy or girl, thought about was the reaction of the first "sweet person" in my life when she opened my valentine at her desk. Beneath the surface of the rhyme, and more importantly, is the obvious and natural occurrence of the analogy, "Sugar is sweet and so are you."

As my granddaughter, Bella, pranced around the backyard astride the long handle of a broom, I knew she visualized much more than a primary schoolgirl frolicking around the yard on a broomstick. She relived the images in the text of *Black Beauty* sketched in her mind. Quite without her awareness, deep in her mind was the delightfully engaging analogy,

Bella is to broomstick as
Harry is to Black Beauty

Of course, her reality was nothing like what I observed. She whinnied as she pranced about, willingly entranced by the relationship between her engaging play and the story she had read over and over again.

The point is a simple one. From our infancy, analogies are an important way that we humans integrate known parts of our lives with novel ones. They arise naturally, not just to me or my granddaughter, Bella, but to all children in families everywhere. Young boys in the hood dart around shirtless in a paved vacant lot, bobbing and swerving to get a sure shot at a waste basket on a high ledge. Yet, that's not what each player envisions. They see that their

junior sized basketball on asphalt : waste basket ::
professional basketball on the Cavaliers' court : NBA goal.

Or there's the young girl alone in a bedroom singing to her heart's content. What's in her mind is

I'm dressed in a tutu with a hairbrush : circle of stuffed animals ::
Taylor Swift in glitter with a microphone : arena of screaming fans.

At first, children are not conscious of the analogies that emerge in life around them, but later on, they understand them, speak them, act them out, and yes, eventually, because they are too old, abandon them. Mary Jane McDonald has long ago faded into the recesses of my childhood memories. Bella has replaced the broomstick with a horse of her own, and her real experiences with Black Beauty lie far beneath her active mental life.

In some entire cultures and in far too many US families, neighborhoods, or social groups, relationships of two unlike things or relationships between contrasting pairs never come up in what students are learning at school. For far too many students, parents, and even educators, school is school, and separately, life is life. This fact does not lessen the importance of analogies in human growth and development. When analogies help children connect novel ideas and experiences with ones they already know, it helps them take charge of expanding their worlds in positive ways. Yet, by and large, student experiences in US K-12 public school education focuses on the right answers and assessments that test one skill or standard at a time on different days, months, or even years.

When students are prompted to respond with analogies in writing, they can occur at several identifiable levels. When students respond at Level 1, it represents the perfect opportunity to open their minds to possibilities at Levels 2 and 3. The core curriculum is the ideal place for helping students see their own level of understanding and expand their understanding of new knowledge more fully.

1	Single-surface feature		A king and a ruler are alike. They wear fancy clothes. They have long robes and shiny shoes. The wear shiny gold medals and crowns, too.
2	Multiple-surface features		A whale and a pig are alike. They are mammals. They have little tiny hairs on their bodies. They have lungs to breathe. Girl whales and pigs have mammary glands for nursing babies. That's why they are called mammals.

3	Surface–internal features		A weather vane and rain gauge are alike. They look very different. The vane is a little pole with arms that turn. The gauge can be on a little pole, but it does not move. They measure the weather. The vane measures the wind, and the gauge measures the rain.

Since humans are natural analogical problem-solvers, it brings to light a serious void in US education. Many district curricula focused on analogies only in high school. That was when the SAT and ACT used analogies as test items. Since that practice is no more, the future of analogies in US education is unclear.

What is clear is the central role that analogous thought plays in adult life in the civilized world. Whether among educated people or not, thinking in analogies provides a world of possible solutions for critical problems that arise, simple or complex. The perils of radiation therapy to rid an otherwise body of a cancerous tumor is to the point. A complex and almost unsolvable problem—Duncker's radiation problem[1]—was resolved by presenting a problem concerning an army and mined roads solved by army leaders without the years of training of a surgical oncologist. When faced with the problem of capturing an enemy city with multiple, mined roads leading into the city, the commander of the unit reasoned that 800 men will set off the charges on any of these roads, while 100 men may not set off the charges on 8 separate roads. And the strategy took the city defenders by surprise as it was hard to determine from which direction the attack was approaching. Back on the operating table, smaller amounts of radiation made it possible to obliterate the tumor without endangering nearby healthy tissue.

Last of all, be wary of any advice couched in the phrase "age appropriate." Countless elementary school teachers I meet steer away from analogies as if they were abstract routines of nanotechnology of the physics of parallel universes. Yet Anne Brown, a researcher at Brown University, discovered otherwise.[2] Preschool children can perform well on problem solving by analogy. A 3-year-old can reason that the hawk-moth caterpillar and the porcupine fish have evolved analogous solutions to warding off predators:

Adult: ... are they the same kind of stories?
Child: Yes, they are the same. . . . Both [the caterpillar and the porcupine] have a mean guy that wants to eat them all up. . . . So **they** get mean and scary so they [the predators] run away!
Adult: They're pretty smart, huh?
Child: Just like me!

Again, the point is simple. There are levels of complexity in analogous relationships, but we are hard set to assign those levels to specific grade levels.

Just about the time you decide analogies in problem solving are not for your second graders, you can be sure you are overlooking a large subset of students like the one from the Brown University study. And do not conclude that all preschoolers with analogous thought have to be a "confident smarty pants" like the 3-year-old in the Brown study. Children are born with the capacity for analogous thought, and when the occasion arises (as in the two stories of the Brown study), they increase their comfort with them. It would be a shame to rule out the work of analogies in the minds of students who are ready and eager to explore them.

Identifying and explaining similarities in novel and known relationships is a major way to propel students through the mass of vocabulary in your core curriculum. The Analogy and Quad Cluster strategies are ideal for directing students through new worlds of novel terms and known terms used in new and technical ways. What better way for elementary students to discover a new meaning for the familiar word, *product*

> *sum : add :: product : multiply* (math)
> *cell phone : product :: car wash : service* (social studies).

The Analogy strategy rolls out like this:

1. List the 4 terms at the analogy at the top of your page.
2. In 1 to 2 sentences, explain how the first pair of words is like the second pair of words (such as antonym, cause-effect, part-to-whole, problem-solution)
3. In 2 to 3 more sentences, explain the full relationship of each pair separately.

The Analogy Strategy for Emerging Writers

With students in grades K-1 and older special students, introduce the four terms on chart paper or interactive board.

- Separate the words with colons and explain that : means *is to* and :: means *as*. Help the students say the analogy as a sentence

  o *over : above :: beside : next to*

- **Over** is to **above** as **beside** is to **next to**. Place the students into PALs of 3 or 4 and let them write a jot list of objects that they see in the room that show how this statement is true.
- PALS group A—*over* and *above : beside and next to*
- Students in this group included sentence and story makers. One of them wrote:

The hall pass is <u>over</u> the lite swich.
The ABCs are <u>above</u> the markr bord.
Hector sits <u>next</u> to Mrs. Cortez.
I sit <u>beside</u> Mrs. Gertrood.

— Juanita P, kindergarten

- Project a slide that shows them that many pairs of words in English mean the same although they look very different. Lead the class to review recent lessons across your curriculum that contain different words that have the same meaning. As you write the analogies for each of the four core subjects, let the students record what you have written. A class of first grade children agreed that

  o story : tale :: setting : location (ELA)
  o *multiply : times :: subtract :: take away* (math)
  o *sound : noise :: dark : shadow* (science)
  o *colonist : settler :: native : Indian* (social studies)
  o *team : side :: sport : game* (physical education)

- The last entry shows how engaged the class was in the activity; several of the students thought of an analogy that concluded just prior to this class discussion.

The variety of ways to position analogies for emerging writers is limitless, I'm sure. Here are a couple I have seen primary teachers create:

- Treasure hunt—You provide a handout for pairs of PALs to complete together based on a class lesson or the classroom environment.

No.	Relationship	First word	:	Second word	Lesson
1	Same	*insect*	:	*bug*	*animals*
2	Opposite	*Snow White*	:	*evil queen*	*fairy tales*
3	Part-to-whole	*coral*	:	*aquarium*	*earth science*
4	Cause-effect	*colonists*	:	*Plymouth*	*history*
5	Member-class	*whale*	:	*mammal*	*life science*

As you observe the pairs' progress, select 3 or 4 of them to present their 2 words to the whole class for them to assess.

Follow-up—Two pairs of PALs huddle to complete the five analogies on a second day. For example, a PALs pair joins the one above to complete an analogy for the first relationship—*insect : bug :: king : ruler.* In this way, students concluded for themselves, "There are words that mean the same in science and in social studies." Later, they saw that synonyms existed in every lesson they ever study.

- Complete the analogy—You provide a simple analogy with the second analogous pair missing, like *hot : cold : _____ : _____*. Each day, analogy PALs take their turn in a rotation of completing the analogy of opposites. The first PALs insert *black : white*; the next PALs insert *tall : short*; the third PALs insert *hard : soft*, and the rotation continues.
- Continue letting groups of 6 students dictate the sentences of an Analogy entry for you to write and place on the wall for them to "read" to others throughout a week or two.

Of course, the best ideas that help your emerging writers thrive in the world of analogies will come from you. When you have developed and tested a good one, tweet a full description of your idea to @RoutledgeEOE.

The Analogy Strategy for Independent Writers

The Analogy strategy for emerging writers focuses primarily on comparing individual surface features (*Queens and kings wear crowns.*), an example of the recall of information (DOK 1). Yet the thoughts of most will move into greater depth of thought:

- They have lots of money. Their kids are called prince and princess—basic reasoning, skills and concepts (DOK 2)
- A prince might become the king. A princess might become the queen—complex reasoning (DOK 3)

That's the power of the Analogy writing strategy; it's nearly impossible to explain analogical relationships without moving into greater depth of knowledge.

With independent writers, the intent of the Analogy writing prompt is quite different. The prompts point to basic reasoning (DOK 2) at minimum and often elicit extended reasoning (DOK 4). As students share with and listen to their PALs, they become aware of increasingly complex relationships. Take this analogy that prompts a response to the standard, "Explain the effects of human activity on the erosion of the earth's surface."

herding cattle : topsoil destruction :: home building : deforestation

Key terms—*depletion, environment, conserve, erosion, habitat, human activity, rain, pollution, soil, soil fertility*

Tamika wrote

Herding cattle is to topsoil destruction as home building is to deforestation. The relationship of each is cause-effect. Herding cattle is a cause of topsoil destruction and soil depletion, and home building is a cause of deforestation. Then *along comes the rain and erosion. Another way they are alike is that they are both human activities that are good for people. People need houses to live in, and ranchers herd cattle to find them food. They both provide jobs for people, too. There a lotsa ways they are alike beside being bad for the environment.*

It seems like Tamika could have written a good deal more about this analogy, yet what she does write sets a solid example for a Level 3 analogy that combines the surface and internal features in the explanation. With independent writers, the procedure for presenting analogies changes.

As with all strategies for constructed response, the Five Key Practices apply.

	Key Practice	Description
I	Quantify your expectations for each constructed response.	Quantify the number of key terms and sentences you expect students to use in their response to every Analogy you prompt.
		• Note that the number of key terms includes words, phrases, symbols, or formulas that students use to explain the relationship of the four terms in the prompt, not the four terms themselves.
		• Expect 3–5 sentences. Fewer sentences rarely explains the analogy fully and more than 5 gets into extended responses.
2	Write your own personal response to Analogy prompts the first couple of times.	Read your model response to the prompt before your students begin writing their entries. Few of them have had prior experience with explaining analogies. You want them to follow your model closely at first. It increases their awareness and mastery of the strategy. Make sure your model exceeds your expectations for student responses.
3	Guide student choices with a simple critical-thinking strategy.	All students read aloud the guidelines in the "Guide for Writing to Learn" for Strategy E. A choral reading of the four guidelines documents that students are engaged in thought about the strategy.
4	Prompt specific PALS strategies with each entry.	Using only the strategy you assign, PALs complete the following sentence stem, "The strength of your writing is/are. . . ." Most often, the Analogy strategy leads to writing in the informative genre.
5	Secure student self-assessment.	When students finish their entries, they complete the three-pronged self-assessment. I. "I used key terms with meaning." 2. "I wrote meaningful sentences." 3. "I used evidence from parts of the text or lesson." Students then read their entries aloud to their PALs and show in their writing evidence of the three scores. PALs agree (√) or question (?) each score.

When you prompt students to construct responses to Analogies, serve them terms, numbers, symbols or formula around seven basic relationships common in our understanding of the world around us.

No.	Relationship	Analogy
1	Part-to-whole	setting : story elements :: conclusion : essay
2a	Antonym	minimum : maximum :: normal : skewed
2b	Synonym	egalitarian : democratic :: dictatorial : autocratic
3	Cause-effect	Gandhi's non-violent protests : India's independence :: 9/11 : invasion of Afghanistan
4	Member-class	improper fractions : rational numbers :: pi : irrational number
5	Class-class	editorial : short story :: nonfiction : fiction
6	Problem-solution	distance/time : speed :: current resistance : voltage
7	Definition (or example)	series : circuit :: radiation : heat

When all of your analogy prompts highlight one of these seven relationships, you

- see analogies more frequently,
- watch analogies become increasingly novel and complex,
- find them more interesting to write than most other strategies,
- see students writing at DOK 3 who have never done so before, and
- discover that analogies differentiate instruction better than other strategies.

By the same token, students

- find that analogies become increasingly easier to analyze and interpret,
- start recognizing analogous relationships on their own,
- sift through new knowledge fluently, and
- revive a strategy that they have used subconsciously from childhood.

Expect the terms that students have explained in analogies to start appearing in class discussions. The terms will appear in their extended writing as well, and when they show up on end of grade tests, students can respond to the test items with confidence.

Exemplar of an Analogy Entry for Independent Writers

Prompt: *Ural Mountains : Russia :: Ayers Rock : Australia.*

Key terms: *aborigines, ancestors, Asia, boundary, central, continent, Europe, Great Victoria Desert*

Expectations: 4–5 key terms; 5–6 sentences

Ural Mountains is to Russia as Ayer's Rock is to Australia. This analogy is a <u>part to</u> whole relationship. The Ural Mountain range is a <u>boundary</u> between <u>Asia</u> and <u>Europe</u>. They are very <u>rocky</u> and <u>bare</u>. Nobody lives in them. They separate East <u>Russia</u> from West Russia. Ayer's Rock is in the center of Australia. It is a reddish, bare rock and nobody lives on it either. Many <u>aborigines</u> visit the rock because they believe it was formed by their <u>ancestors</u>. It is in the <u>Great Victoria Desert</u>.

— Jimmy J, grade 7

Variations on Presenting an Analogy

So as you look for ways to employ the Analogy strategy for activating or summarizing key concepts in learning, consider the following progression of constructed responses to analogy prompts with your students:

- First off, serve up an analogy of synonyms. Students have met and practiced identifying words that are the same and different since kindergarten. Use this accessible prompt to set students' response to all analogies with a standard two-sentence answer. For example, when students read the analogy

    observe : analyze :: overlook : ignore

    the first sentence restates the analogy in a sentence:

    Observe is to analyze as overlook is to ignore.

    The second sentence identifies the relationship common to the pairs.

    The first two words mean the same, and the second two words mean the same.

    Sentences 3 through 5 and beyond explain why the writer believes the pairs relate to one another in similar ways. When students use this two-sentence formula, they have

    o Made it clear that they have interpreted the analogy as it was written,
    o Taken charge of their response,
    o Committed to one common relationship between the pairs, and
    o Have three or more sentences remaining to explain their choice fully.

- Second, let students learn to identify the part-to-whole relationship in an analogy by doing. No direct teaching; give students a chance to identify the relationship. There's a good chance that more than one of them will.

    evaporation : water cycle :: crust : earth

- After students have met most of the seven relationships, start serving them analogies that are more open to interpretation. For example, in the study of the human body,

hand : arm :: foot : leg

can be interpreted as part-to-whole

Hands on humans are on the end of their arms, and feet are on the end of their legs.

In the standards of life science in the early grades, the description of the human skeletal system implies this relationship.

Later, in middle grades life science, students may interpret the relationship as member-to-class.

Hands are members of the class of bones that make up the arm. Feet are members of the class of bones we call our legs.

Some middle grade students have shown a different take on the analogy and argued that the relationship was class-to-class.

Hand and arm represent two classes of bones in the human body. The hand has 27 bones for small, complex movements. The arm belongs to a class of bones of large, simple movements. Likewise, the foot and leg represent the same two classes. A foot contains 26 bones for small, complex movements, while the leg is designed for larger, simple moves. These are two of the important classes of bones in the human skeletal system.

Actually, your students will help you discover open analogies. You will prompt an analogy that has one relationship based on your understanding of a course standard. The member-to-class example of *hand* to *arm* is a classic example. When a middle school science teacher assigned this prompt, she received an alternate response from a student who saw the relationship as class-to-class. When such insight emerges, it is a clear sign of extended reasoning (DOK 4). It is time to share this response with the class and encourage others to think "out of the box."

- Conclude with student-created analogies, ones based on a core standard you have taught. The caveat here is that the students may define the relationship in their analogies in a novel way. The seven relationships are not sacred. So be prepared. The following chart provides relationships that students claimed for their analogies. I have inserted a corresponding list of the seven strategies. As you can see, in many cases, the relationship students highlight in their analogies amount to a more specific instance of the more global seven. In other words, students are a source of increasingly engaging and rich examples of analogies that explore the seven basic relationships. Note how many of the analogies relate one standard to another standard, to current events, or to their everyday lives.

	Student Analogy	Stated Relationship	...an instance of...
1	*fly : airplane :: drive : car*	action-to-object	definition (7)
2	*Gable : Leigh :: Arnaz : Ball*	actor-to-actress pairs	class-to-class (5)
3	*David Suchet : mystery :: Meg Ryan : comedy*	actor-to-genre	member-to-class (4)
4	*Twain : Tom Sawyer :: Lee : To Kill a Mockingbird*	author-to-novel	member-to-class (4)
5	*fleas : Black Death :: mosquito : malaria*	causes determined long after the event	cause-effect (3)
6	*inflation : deflation :: frail : strong*	antonyms	antonym-synonym (2)
7	*mammal : porpoise :: fish : catfish*	category-to-example	member-to-class (4)
8	*tropical : hot :: polar : cold*	characteristic	definition (7)
9	*Rogers : Somewhere over the Rainbow :: Newton : Amazing Grace*	composer-to-song	definition (7)
10	*Bieber : pop :: Presley : rock*	singer-to-genre	definition (7)
11	*mist : heavy fog :: drizzle : tropical storm*	degree of characteristic	synonym (2b)
12	*paint : painting :: carve : sculpture*	effort and result	cause-effect (3)
13	*knife : cut :: ruler : measure*	item-to-purpose	definition (7)
14	*This war is right because we are American : This war is wrong because they are Iranian :: I am America (And So Can You) : Dead Lawyers (and Other Pleasant Thoughts)*	non-sequiturs	member-to-class, definition (4,7)
15	*shovel : garden tool :: microphone : amplifier*	object-to-function	definition (7)
16	*house : garage :: swimming pool : diving board*	object-to-related object	part-to-whole (1)
17	*poet : ballad :: baker : croissant*	product-to-worker	definition (7)
18	*No matter how you feel, get up, dress up and show up : inspire :: Don't put all of your eggs in one basket : warn*	sequitur-to-purpose	definition (7)

(Continued)

	Student Analogy	Stated Relationship	. . . an instance of . . .
19	*Life is life and we humans get to live it : sequitur :: Life is life and fun is fun, and when goldfish die, it's very quiet : non-sequitur*	sequitur-to-non-sequitur	member-to-class, definition (4,7)
20	*The rock browned over time : sequitur :: The rock breathed in new life : non-sequitur*	sequitur-to-non-sequitur	member-to-class, definition (4,7)
21	*could have been : past perfect :: may have been : present perfect*	Tense	definition (7)
22	*salt : pepper :: bacon : eggs*	things that go together	definition (7)
23	*word processor : writer :: voice : singer*	tool-to-worker	definition (7)
24	*Golden Retriever : dog :: salmon : fish*	type	member-to-class (4)
25	*white-tailed : deer :: Tennessee Walker : horse*	breed-to-animal	member-to-class (4)

- Field trips or common experiences are perfect opportunities for students to uncover analogies for themselves. Teachers have asked students to identify analogies as they spend time in a normal activity. These analogies appeared in a class after student went out for dinner.

  o *A Coney Island : hotdog :: a T-bone : beef steak (member-to-class)*
  o *napkin : table :: chef : waiter* (class-to-class)
  o *menu : wine list :: entree : dessert* (class-to-class)
  o *entree : filling :: server : efficient* (definition)
  o *Bananas Foster : crème brulee :: merlot : pinot noir* (class-to-class)
  o *twice-baked potatoes : hash browns :: Granny Smith : Fuji* (class-to-class)

Analogies and Course Standards

A second progression in presenting analogies allows you to move from constructed responses to a single standard, to multiple standards, and to students' everyday experiences. This intentional progress surely increases students' depth and breadth of understanding (DOK). It boosts their awareness of connections between what they write and what they already know from class lessons, reading texts, current events, or everyday life.

Note how the progressions of analogies parallels that of Quad Clusters in the previous chapter. These two strategies work in tandem to provide a most rigorous, varied acquisition of the vocabulary of the subjects you teach. The intent here is to show how the Quad Cluster and Analogy strategies allow you to fine-tune your attention to differentiated learning among your students. You will see some students benefit more from responding to Quad Clusters, some from Analogies.

Emerging Writer

Analogies within a Single Standard

It is easy to vary the analogies drawn on terms from within a standard using the seven relationships.

Current standard from Life Science: Understand how to investigate the characteristics and basic needs of plants and animals

- o *root : bush :: hooves : horse* (part-to-whole)
- o *leaves : flower :: grain : cow* (cause-to-effect)
- o *lion : cat :: wolf : dog* (class-to-class: wild to domestic)

Previous standard from Earth Science: How to observe, measure, and communicate weather data to see patterns in weather and climate

- o *mercury : water :: thermometer : rain gauge* (class-to-class within each pair; part-to-whole the first words of each pair and the second words of each pair)
- o *cloudy : wet :: sunny : dry* (definition)
- o *dark clouds : rain :: 20°F and precipitation : snow* (cause-to-effect)

Analogies across Standards

When you begin including terms from more than one standard, the engagement in the writing increases. The relationships become more interesting and complex, too. They bring richness and variety to the Analogy strategy.

Current standard from Life Science: Understand how to investigate the characteristics and basic needs of plants and animals

Previous standard from Earth Science: How to observe, measure, and communicate weather data to see patterns in weather and climate

- o *mercury : thermometer :: water : plants* (part-to-whole)
- o *maple : carbon dioxide :: rain gauge : precipitation* (members of a class, one basic need)
- o *nutrients : blossom :: cold front : temperature drop* (cause-to-effect)

Analogies Related to Everyday Life

The interesting relationships among terms continue to unfold when students connect their explanations of analogies to current events or their day-to-day lives.

Current standard from Life Science: Understand how to investigate the characteristics and basic needs of plants and animals

Everyday life of the writer at home: Awareness of characteristics and basic needs of students in family life. Human needs are included in the study of basic needs of animals.

- *roots : bush :: steering wheel : car* (part-to-whole)
- *carbon dioxide : rose :: junk food : sickness* (cause-effect)
- *daffodil : flower :: Uncle Javier : extended family* (member-to-class)

Exemplar of an Emerging Writer

Key terms—*domestic, female, mammal, male, pack (wolf family), pet, pride (lion family), wild lion : cat :: wolf : dog*

Teacher model (written with students and read after the writing):

Lion is to cat as wolf is to dog. The relationship of each is domestic to wild (class-to-class). Lions are wild cats that live in prides. Cats we know make good pets and live in our houses with us. Wolves are wild dogs that live in packs. Wolves are not safe to be around. Dogs make great pets and are often part of people's families.

Oral student exemplar that exceeds expectations:

Lion is to cat as wolf is to dog. Lions are big and angry. A wolf is to, but it is smaller. I never saw a real lion. I wouldn't want to. Cats and dogs are nice. Maxwell [family dog] slept with me. I wouldn't want a lion on my bed.

— Timothy B, pre-kindergarten

Independent Writers
Analogies within a Single Standard

It is easy to vary the analogies drawn on terms from within a standard using the seven relationships. Here are three examples for a standard in math.

Current standard from math: Identify parts of an expression using mathematical terms (sum, term, product, factor, quotient, coefficient); view one or more parts of an expression as a single entity.

- *parentheses : linear expression :: factor : multiplication* (part-to-whole)
- *term : coefficient :: dividend : divisor* (member : class)
- *parts : single entity :: dividend and divisor : problem* (definition)

Analogies across Standards

When analogies compare relationships among words from two different standards, the thinking of student writers broadens and deepens. These examples illustrate exactly how.

Current standard from math: Identify parts of an expression using mathematical terms (sum, term, product, factor, quotient, coefficient); view one or more parts of an expression as a single entity.

Previous standard from math: Write expressions that record operations with numbers and with letters standing for numbers.

1. *2 (8 + 7) : (7 + 8) 2 :: 5 (3 + 7) : 5 (y + 7)* (synonyms)
2. *letters : variable :: number : constant* (definition)

Analogies Related to Everyday Life

Current standard from World History: Analyze the relationship among Christianity, Judaism, and Islam.

Previous standard from World History: Explain the development and impact of Hinduism and Buddhism on India and subsequent diffusion of Buddhism.

- *Hinduism : Judaism :: Mehta : Goldberg* (class-to-class: two world religions and surnames of two neighbors who are members of those religions)
- *Quran : Bible :: user manual : cookbook* (class-to-class: sacred texts that serve as religious guides)
- *religious authority : freedom of belief :: statement of faith : pledge of allegiance* (antonyms: religious vs. non-religious)

The interesting relationships among terms continue to unfold when you include terms from everyday life. Inserting everyday terms into analogies ensures that students store new knowledge securely in structures of prior knowledge. Neuroscience research suggests that new knowledge tied to prior knowledge does not wash away from students' minds during the next night's sleep (see http://www.nature.com/neuro/journal/v15/n11/full/nn.3238.html).

Current standard from US History: The student will analyze the impact of territorial expansion and population growth and the impact of this growth in the early decades of the new nation.

Element: Describe the construction of the Erie Canal, the rise of New York City, and the development of the nation's infrastructure.

- *tow path : standard gauge trackage :: Ferris wheel : rollercoaster* (class-to-class)
- *Erie Canal : Albany, New York :: I-70 : Denver, Colorado* (definition)

Element: Describe the reasons for and importance of the Monroe Doctrine.

- *Monroe Doctrine of 1823 : NAFTA of 1994 :: Title IX requirements for sports : 19th amendment to the US Constitution* (synonyms, class-to-class, definition) o *War of 1812 : Monroe Doctrine of 1823 :: Title IX requirements for sports : girls high school soccer team* (cause-effect)

Benefits Teachers Attribute to the Use of the Analogy Strategy

The Analogy strategy presents extraordinary help for students in fine-tuning domain-specific and academic vocabulary for learning.

- A strong vocabulary builder:

  o "First graders see analogies as big-deal puzzles. When they figure one of them out, their faces beam with accomplishment." (Georgia grade 1 teacher)

  o "My own rocky history with analogies kept me from seeing that analogies came naturally to students. My classes took the strategy in stride when I introduced it in October. Amazing!" (Georgia grade 6 math teacher)

  o "I feared analogies until a consultant explained that analogies on tests focused on correct answers, not the explanation of why the answers were logical. It relieved all of my anxiety about analogies, and my students use the language of science better than ever." (Tennessee grade 3 teacher)

  o "I use the single surface feature analogy with concepts I introduce to my biology students. The surface-internal feature analogies come later. When the level of complexity fits the students' degree of familiarity with a concept, I literally see them absorbing the vocabulary." (Georgia grade 10 biology teacher)

- A favorite strategy of students:

  o "Last year, There was no evidence of analogies in the school; now they are the favorite strategy that students choose to post as exemplars." (South Dakota elementary school principal)

  o "I have encouraged students to bring quad clusters and acrostics to school. Was I ever surprised when students started bringing in analogies on their own; many of them were right on the mark for the standards we were studying." (Georgia grade 7 ELA teacher)

Summing Up

The Analogies strategy partners with the Quad Cluster to offer a double-barrel approach to bolstering students' use of the vocabulary of a course of study.

Furthermore, early rounds of state assessments of core standards show that students are asked to construct a response to how a specific key term or phrase is used in a test reading passage. Emerging writers dictate to their teachers the sentences in a constructed response to an Analogy, and they respond well to games that require them to identify or offer analogies for objects, actions, procedures, or events in their school environment or curriculum. Independent writers are encouraged to

- move beyond developing one relationship that applies to both pairs in the analogy,
- solve analogies that span the standards of the curriculum, and
- relate their new knowledge to prior knowledge from the daily lives or the world around them.

Additionally, independent writers are tasked with creating analogies based on course standards and work in PALS to identify analogies hidden in the course curriculum. As students meet and contribute analogies to the archive of analogies their teachers maintain, they are expected to include words from two vocabulary lists: words that are academic (used in any subject area) and domain-specific (used only in a subject area).

With completion of the section of two strategies that focus on word study, they are ready to move onto strategies that require elaboration (chapters 9 and 10) and argument (chapter 11).

Notes

1. Gick and Holyoak, "Duncker's Radiation Problem, and Transfer," 1980, www. csi.ucd.ie/staff/fcummins/CogModels/duncker.html
2. Brown, A. L. (1989). Analogical learning and transfer: What develops? In S. Vosniadou & A. Ortony (Eds.), *Similarity and analogical reasoning* (pp. 369–412). London: Cambridge University Press.

Chapter 9

From General to Specific
(Telling to Showing)

For decades, ELA teachers admonished students each year to return to their writing and replace general nouns and verbs with more specific ones. I did this frequently my first year teaching seventh graders back in the 1970s. The decades have shown precious little benefit from all that talking, cajoling, motivating, and borderline threatening.

This short chapter pays additional tribute to the Individualized Language Arts (ILA) writing project, a nationally validated program in New Jersey. Development and dissemination were funded partly by the Milliken Family Foundation. In one state alone, ILA was a familiar term among educators in every public school district from 1980–2000. The use of the program coincided with a rise in that state's student performance on tests of written expression. A review of the impact data from those years shows that the ILA strategy that impacted student performance most noticeably was Slotting. Time passed, and the ILA teacher manuals have disappeared, but the Slotting strategy is a definite standout in the toolkit of teachers to enhance the rigor of constructed responses for learning in every subject area.

Interestingly, when you locate *slotting* in a dictionary, the connection to writing is unclear.

> a narrow, elongated depression, groove, notch, slit, or aperture, especially a narrow opening for receiving or admitting something, as a coin or a letter

Yet the connection is quite a powerful one.

The Slotting Strategy for Emerging Writers

For emerging writers, schedule 2 consecutive days for constructing responses with the Slotting strategy. On Day 1, the students do the thinking and you (the teacher) do the writing. Simply serve up a sentence with general or vague nouns and verbs slotted (underlined). Each slot provides an "opening for receiving" more specific words. Here's an example from a first grade classroom projected on an interactive board.

A <u>man</u> <u>picked up</u> a few <u>items</u> from the <u>store</u>.

For each general word slotted, the teacher solicited from students a jot list of more specific words that could replace it and a sharper mental picture. For *man*, the students offered a torrent of suggestions, and their teacher wisely asked after each suggestion, "Does that make a better picture in our minds?" Suggestions like *nice man, person,* and *human* were rejected by the students until the class agreed on the five substitutes below and their teacher listed them on the interactive white board. They followed the same process for the other three slotted words. When they worked on *store*, their teacher asked them to check the words from the first three lists to make sure that the words for *store* could fit with some of them. So when the jot lists contained words that the students agreed helped make a clearer pictures in their minds, Day 1 was complete.

A <u>man</u>	<u>picked up</u>	a few <u>items</u>	from the <u>store</u>.
farmer	bought	groceries	supermarket
daddy	charged	video games	mall
grandpa	borrowed	snacks	C-store
fireman	stole	televisions	clothing store
robber	purchased	Sunday shoes	drug store

On Day 2, it was time for the students to take over the thinking and the writing. Their task? Write two new versions of the slotted sentence, using one word from each of the lists in each sentence. Here the teacher encouraged them to use even better words that came to their minds than the ones on the list. One student wrote

The robber stole a few televisions at the mall.
The fireman purchased snacks from the drug store.

— Carly D, grade 1

Carly represents most of the first graders who slot for more specific words. A smaller group of students take the task a bit further. Jacque took his teacher's advice and added some of his own, more specific words. It is clear from his sentences that he understands how to change sentences with vague and general words into ones filled with specific words.

The firemen bought a bunch of sweet and salty snacks at the C-store. The soldiers borrowed a few grocery carts from the supermarket to carry their bags. They took them back.

— Jacque H, grade 1

The guide for the Slotting strategy reads like this:

1. In the sentence your teacher provides, create a list of words beneath each slot.
2. Write a sentence that uses words from each list.
3. Use different words from each list to write a second sentence.
4. Write a third sentence that uses new words that come from your mind.

As with all strategies for constructed response, the Five Key Practices apply.

	Key Practice	Description
1	Quantify your expectations for each constructed response.	Quantify the number of sentences you expect students to create in their response a Slotting prompt. • For emerging writers, expect 1–2 sentences; encourage use of additional words. • "Additional" includes words, phrases, numbers, and symbols. • For independent writers, consider moving the Slotting strategy into revision of extended writing.
2	Write your own personal response to Slotting prompts the first couple of times.	Read your model response to the prompt before your students begin writing their entries. Slotting is new to most students. It is wise for them to follow your model closely at first. It increases their awareness and mastery of the strategy. Make sure your model exceeds your expectations for student responses.
3	Guide student choices with a simple critical-thinking strategy.	All students read aloud the guidelines in the "Guide for Writing to Learn" for strategy U. When students are saying the words aloud, you know their minds are focused on the strategy.
4	Prompt specific PALS strategies with each entry.	Using the PALS strategy you assign, PALs complete the following Sentence Stem, "The strength of your writing is...." *Voice, pictures, flow* provide the most useful three choices for a response.

Key Practice		Description
5	Secure student self-assessment.	When students finish their entries, they complete two of the statements for self-assessment. 1. "I used key terms with meaning." 2. "I wrote meaningful sentences." Students then read their entries aloud to their PALs and show evidence in their writing of the three scores. PALs agree (√) or question (?) each score.

The Slotting Strategy for Independent Writers

As students' sentences written with the Slotting strategy show greater creativity and extension in thought, it is time to put their slotting skill to work in their extended (multi-paragraph) writing. While students' revision of their extended writing is beyond the scope of this book, it is important to see that the Slotting strategy for constructed responses equips emerging writers with a marked sense of revision as they become independent writers. The following procedure is based on Revision Strategy 2: Slotting for Better Word Choices in *A Writing Cycle for Writer's Workshop*, pp. R-15:

> **Slotting** is a simple, self-directed revision strategy for independent writers to use in their extended writing. In a mini-lesson, guide students through the Slotting strategy described for emerging writers above. Then prompt them to apply this basic process to a first draft they have written.

1. Use the Picture Killer wall chart (pp. 38–39) to help identify the vague words in your first draft.
2. Underline at least 1 or 2 vague words in each sentence of your first draft.
3. Circle 10 nouns and verbs that you know you can slot for better word choice. Then number the circled words 1 through 10.
4. Write the circled words by the corresponding numbers on a clean sheet of paper.
5. Work with an assigned buddy to help each other replace the first two slotted words with phrases that create clearer pictures in your mind.
6. Work alone to slot better word choices on the remaining circled words.
7. Use a thesaurus or words from the Picture Maker wall chart to help. In a word processor, right-click on the marked words and select more specific synonyms that fit the pictures in your mind.
8. It is important to replace some words with phrases or clauses to make your thoughts clear for readers. Don't hesitate to use all the

specific words that come to your mind to improve your first draft for your readers to enjoy.

9. When you enjoy revising your first draft, your readers will enjoy reading the revised draft.

Eighth grader Antoine followed the above steps in slotting for better word choices in his paragraph. Although he created the assigned 10 words in the first paragraph, he continued to add more details to his writing in later paragraphs.

The people wanted to be free. They wrote the Declaration of Independence. It persuaded the people to organize and fight. Men left their homes and jobs and joined the army. They said they would give their lives to be free. Some of them actually did. The people that lived made a new country for themselves.

On a clean sheet of paper, he slotted for better word choice. The words Antoine used from the Picture Maker wall chart are underlined.

1. people → leaders of the 13 British colonies in America
2. wanted → met together to make a plan
3. free → get rid of King George who was insane
4. they → 55 leaders of the colonies met and
5. wrote → decided what to put in
6. It → This document became very important and
7. organize → form armies with generals like George Washington
8. said → gave speeches to say
9. lived → survived the revolution
10. made → created a government for the people and by the people

His introductory paragraph looked like this after he revised it using the Slotting strategy. Note that Antoine made some additional revisions as he create his final draft:

The leaders of the 13 British colonies in America met together to make a plan. They wanted to be rid of King George of England who was insane. 55 leaders of the colonies met and decided what to put in the Declaration of Independence. This document became very important and persuaded the people to form armies with generals like George Washington and fight. Men left their homes and jobs and joined the army and gave their lives to be free. The leaders gave speeches and wrote papers about freedom. Many of them actually did die. The people that survived the revolution created a government for the people <u>and</u> called it the United States.

Notice the difference between emerging and independent writers. Emerging writers tend to replace single words with more single words. Independent writers replace words with descriptive phrases. When some students make such graphic improvements, they often continue to make improvements throughout their first drafts.

The Slotting strategy has its use with simple reading texts as well. As you watch, your students fill in the details of a text that presents information about which they have some prior knowledge.

Martin Luther King Jr. was a leader. He lived from 1929 to 1968. Americans honor him in January with a national holiday. King grew up in the southern part of the United States. At that time, laws treated African American people differently from white people. African Americans were forced to sit in the back of buses. They also had to use separate bathrooms and water fountains. When King was older, he worked to change those laws. As a result, equal rights laws were passed.

On a clean sheet of paper, tenth grader Maria slotted for better word choice. The words Maria used from the Picture Maker wall chart are underlined.

1. leader → natural born organizer <u>and</u> motivator <u>of</u> people
2. He → This son <u>of</u> a Baptist preacher <u>from</u> Atlanta
3. honor → remember his legacy <u>as</u> civil rights leader <u>for</u> all people
4. they → 55 leaders <u>of</u> the colonies met <u>and</u>
5. grew → was raised <u>in</u> a parsonage <u>in</u> several cities
6. laws → Jim Crow laws <u>and</u> social patterns left over <u>from before</u> the civil war
7. white people → people <u>who</u> no longer owned them, <u>but</u> treat them <u>as</u> inferiors <u>in</u> many ways.
8. sit → were forced to give their seats up <u>after</u> working hard all day <u>and</u> move <u>to</u> the back <u>of</u> the bus <u>or</u> just stand
9. use → hunt around <u>to</u> find unequal,
10. he → this dynamic <u>and</u> skillful leader <u>of</u> non-violent tactics
11. change → replace unfair <u>and</u> prejudicial
12. were passed → slowly progressed <u>through</u> months <u>of</u> planning, negotiation <u>and</u> arm-twisting <u>to</u> be signed into law <u>by</u> President L.B. Johnson.

What an accomplishment for this eighth grade writer. Although she added little that is not already well known by US middle school students, her final draft began like this:

Martin Luther King Jr. was a natural born organizer <u>and</u> motivator <u>of</u> people. This son <u>of</u> a Baptist preacher <u>from</u> Atlanta lived from 1929 to 1968. Americans remember his legacy <u>as</u> civil rights leader <u>for</u> all people <u>in</u> January with a national holiday. King was raised <u>in</u> a parsonage <u>in</u> several cities <u>around</u> the southern part <u>of</u> the United States. At that time, Jim Crow laws <u>and</u> social patterns left over <u>from before</u> the civil war treated African American people differently <u>from</u> people <u>who</u> no longer owned them, <u>but</u> treat them <u>as</u> inferiors <u>in</u> many ways. African Americans were forced <u>to</u> give their seats up <u>after</u> working hard all day <u>and</u> move <u>to</u> the back <u>of</u> the bus <u>or</u> just stand <u>in</u> the back <u>of</u> buses. They also had <u>to</u> hunt around <u>to</u> find unequal, separate bathrooms and water fountains. When King was older, this dynamic <u>and</u> skillful leader <u>of</u> non-violent tactics worked to replace unfair <u>and</u> prejudicial laws. As a result, equal rights laws slowly progressed <u>through</u> months <u>of</u> planning, negotiation <u>and</u> arm-twisting <u>to</u> be signed <u>into</u> law <u>by</u> President L.B. Johnson.

Although Maria didn't maintain this degree of rich slotting use to the end of the reading passage, she did continue to move at least one noun or verb from general to specific in each sentence. Notice the difference in *voice, pictures,* and *flow* of the passage with Maria's revisions in the opening paragraph. When she was asked how and why she such thorough revisions, she simply quipped, "That reading passage needed a lot of help."

There is no doubt that when independent writers slot for these kinds of improvements in other people's writing, they will have practiced creating sentences that will carry over to their writing on demand.

Benefits Teachers Attribute to the Use of the Slotting Strategy

The Slotting strategy provides a simple, student-friendly way to condition students to more specific word choices in the sentences they write. Hear what teachers say and what their students say.

- The Slotting strategy "teaches revision by doing" with writers:
  - "My first graders see slotting as puzzles to solve. Creating new sentences with better words brings big smiles to their faces." (Georgia grade 1 teacher)
  - "Slotting makes my students think, 'Do I need the word number, or do I really mean digit, numeral, figure or integer?' There are times it makes a big difference." (Georgia grade 5 math teacher)

- "I never heard of slotting and thought a strategy from 1970s could not apply to my kids. When our instructional coordinator chose my class to demonstrate it for other teachers, my kids loved right-clicking the word and picking a better synonym. Several asked, 'Can we three words instead of just one.'" (South Carolina grade 6 teacher)
- "I thought Acrostics, Quad Clusters and Analogies were the vocabulary builders in Chemistry. Now I'm adding slotting to the mix to give students a strategy for choosing just the precise word. That's huge in science writing." (Georgia grade 10 chemistry teacher)

- A favorite strategy of students:

  - "In conferencing with a student about slotting, I heard her say, 'I just love to make sentences grow bigger.' I thought you'd like to know." (South Carolina grade 1 teacher)
  - "Slotting is the best strategy for students working in pairs. Slotting buddies really help each other set a procedure for picking the best specific word for their response." (South Dakota grade 6–7 ELA teacher)
  - "After I moved on for two weeks to other strategies for constructed responses, several of my sixth graders asked, 'Can we slot today?' I wasn't expecting that, so we slotted that day and at least twice a month to the end of the school year. They details in their writing shows!" (Georgia grade 6 teacher)
  - "Setting up sentences for slotting was a good bit of work for me at first, but when I saw how much the kids enjoyed it and how their word choice improved in their writing, I was OK." (Mississippi grade 1–2 parochial school teacher)

Summing Up

The Slotting strategy can provide frequent practice replacing general terms that bring clear pictures back to writers' minds with specific terms that create pictures in readers' minds. With emerging writers, replacements most often include one specific term for a general one. With independent writers, replacement terms grow to phrases dotted with picture makers from the Picture Makers chart (pp. 38–39). When you model the strategy fully in your own writing and refer to writing as a word or language game, you'll see more and more students engage themselves in playing this productive game.

It is interesting to note that as students grow in their engaged word and language play, more and more specific words and phrases begin appearing in their first drafts. And the Slotting strategy is an early strategy in the nurture of revision among students in *A Writing Cycle for Writer's Workshop* (grades K-2). In short, the Slotting strategy enhances

- more and more specific word choices,
- sentence expansion, and
- students' revision of first drafts at the word and sentence level.

Chapter 10 rounds out the pair of chapters that focus on the elaboration of words and sentences.

Chapter 10

Analyzing for Meaning

> Hi, Mom; what's for snack?
>
> Your favorite; but first, how was your day?
>
> Juanita thought a moment, then blurted out, If you give a moose a muffin. . . .
>
> Patiently, her mother waited a good while, then asked, If I give a moose a muffin, what?
>
> I forgot, Juanita admits.
>
> Fortunately, within minutes, she and her mom enjoy a small bowl of fresh, ripe, sliced mangoes.

Actually, Juanita forgot what the text of a favorite picture book *said*. She very likely did not yet understand what the text *meant*. Since she had no central idea on which to secure her understanding, in three short hours, she *forgot*. Focusing on what texts say is not unusual for emerging writers, and fortunately, they can learn to analyze text for meaning. The Story Reporting strategy is one certain way that emerging writers can mine the meaning from reading texts or class lessons. What I Thought You Taught serves a similar purpose for independent writers.

Story Reporting as a Search for Meaning with Emerging Writers

The Story Reporting strategy helps emerging writers in a number of specific ways. It

- gives them a procedure for recalling the key words in a story,
- coaches students to sound out words and spell them as they sound, and
- helps them acquire a better sense of "wordness" by prompting them to list one word under another.

At first, the strategy involves your whole classroom. We'll use Juanita's new favorite story *If You Give a Moose a Muffin* to illustrate the process of story reporting. First, lead the class in brainstorming possible key words to include in their writing. With each word suggested by one of the students in the class, ask, "Is this a really important word, or is it just a detail?" Once your class agrees that *moose* is a key word, tell them you will help them write down the sounds so they hear when they pronounce the word *moose*. Lead them in saying the word together aloud and ask,

1. What's the first sound you hear when we said *moose*? When some of them say *M*, direct them to write the letter *M* at the top of their paper. After most students have written their letters, show them how you wrote an uppercase *M* at the top of your page and coach them as they create an *M* on their pages.

2. Continue asking the class what sound they heard second. Have them repeat the word *moose* aloud together so they can listen more carefully.

3. If someone says *U,* ask the class if they heard a *U* sound second. When they all agree, direct them to write the letter *U* to the right of the letter *M* on their pages. Do not show the class your model *MU* on your page. Show it only to those students who absolutely need to have the help in placing the *U* to the right of *M.*

4. Repeat steps 2 and 3 until students agree that they have written enough letters to remember the sounds in *moose.* Unless a student recalls how *moose* was spelled from the picture book, they may conclude the *mus* will help them remember the word.

5. Now, let's repeat steps 1 through 4 for the second keyword: muffin. When your students have all written *MAFN* to represent the sounds in *muffin,* point to the letters *MUS* and ask them what *MUS* helps them remember.

6. Then ask them what *MAFN* helps them remember.

When they remember these first two important words as planned, follow this 5-step procedure with up to 5 additional key terms, enough terms for them to capture the plot structure of the story, in this case, a circular structure. The story begins and ends with giving the moose a muffin. With your coaching and practice, students increase the pace at which they select and write out the sounds that they hear when they pronounce 5 to 8 key words. These words, then, help them report the story to a PAL, a small group of PALs, the whole class, and eventually their significant adults at home.

Teacher model—The first time you write with the students, spell the words with just the sounds that the students identify for the class to use just like you see the students doing on their pages.

MUS
MAFN

JAM
SWETR
SHETS
BLACK BERI
MAFN

Note that the teacher limited the number of key words to seven. Seven words were enough to identify the circular plot structure that will help kindergartens understand what the story *means*. Unlike Juanita, the writers in this class reported that, "If you give a moose a muffin,

"... he will just want more and more." (Cory)
"... the story will happen all over again." (Koreshia)
"... it will make him want something else, and then he will want something else, and it won't ever stop." (Minesh)

And all three of these student writers were ready to explain how their seven words show you exactly what the story means. When students understand the plot structure of a story, they have moved beneath the words in the story to the story's meaning. **Note:** Story Reporting is published orally, so written drafts are not available to include.

Plot Structures and Meaning in Stories

In "Story Skeletons: Teaching Plot Structure with Picture Books," Shutta Crum categorizes stories in structures of plots that authors use to tell their stories in picture books. She offers her categories to help elementary students, grades 3 and above, in organizing their own creative stories. There is, however, more power in understanding plot structures than Crum suggests. They can help students understand stories that fit these categories at a deeper level much sooner than grade 3. When students identify the plot structure of a story, they have moved beyond what a story *says* to what it *means* like in the example, *If You Give a Moose a Muffin*.

Here is an example of how to introduce a second plot structures.

Every story we read in this class has a plot structure just like *If You Give a Moose a Muffin*. Story structures are very much like the structure inside our bodies. Someone tell us what the bones in our bodies that help us stand, sit, and move are called. When you hear a student suggest *skeleton*, continue. Our skeletons help us look like ourselves and help us do all the moving that we need. Stories have skeletons, too. When you see what the skeleton of a story looks like as you listen or read, you will understand the story better and deeper, and you will remember it for a long time.

Yesterday, we read the story of "The Tailor" together. (Some versions of the same plot structure are *Something from Nothing* or *Bit by Bit*.)

Remember, "The Tailor" presents the story of a poor, little old tailor who takes the scraps of cloth left over from making nice things for his customers to create something nice for himself. He stitches several pieces together into a large square to make himself a coat. As the coat starts to wear out, he cuts it down to make a (*jacket*). [Invite the students fill in the blank aloud all together.] Later, as more cloth wears away, he makes a (*vest*), then a (*cap*), a (*pocket*), and finally, a (*cloth-covered button*).

As the tailor wears out each piece of clothing, he creates a smaller one. The skeleton of the story is large-to-small or more-to-less.

The story wouldn't work any other way. When they think large-to-small, they know the clothing cannot move from coat to cap to jacket. It must be laid out as it is in order to work. The moral or lesson of the story easily tumbles out the mouths of the students.

- *Don't throw old clothes away.*
- *You can use things again . . . and again.*
- *Recycle pieces of clothes.*

Below is a list of some basic plot structures, along with picture books that use those structures. Reading or listening to these stories will help students identify other stories like them. In a real sense, other stories like them have similar meanings.

Cumulative or Toppling Stories

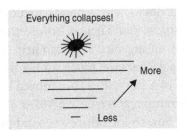

This Is the Teacher by R. G. Greene presents a classic example of a cumulative structure. Like the traditional tale "The House That Jack Built," the cumulative plot structure repeats plot elements and characters in the text as the story progresses, until the whole structure collapses from its own weight—usually with humorous results. In *This Is the Teacher*, students rush into class late, drop their lunches in the cafeteria, spill the ant farm, and let loose a snake during science lab. To be sure, the story is an entertaining comedy of errors, and the collapse does not occur until the teacher plops down and closes her eyes at home. The bee in Patricia Polacco's *Enzo's Splendid Gardens* and the surprising character,

Carol Mack, in *The Cake that Mack Ate* provide other clear examples of cumulative stories.

Decreasing Stories

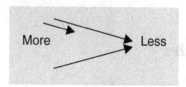

Preceded by the traditional tales, "The Tailor" and "Ten Little Monkeys," Carol Schaefer's *The Biggest Soap* follows a decreasing plot structure. In an unidentified town in Micronesia, Kessy sets off to buy "the biggest soap" for laundry day. Since he uses it to help friends and family he meets all along the way home, he delivers barely enough the soap left for his Mama to clean the week's laundry.

Increasing Stories

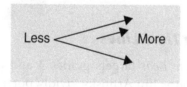

Traditional tales that use the increasing story structure include "The Little Old Lady who Swallowed a Fly." In the same structure, Bill Grossman's *My Little Sister Ate One Hare* is a counting story with an increasing plot structure. The items on the sister's menu grow more outrageous until the story finally reaches a satisfying conclusion (read it to find out). Unlike cumulative stories that are largely repetitious and often pure silliness, increasing plot stories proceed logically to a reasonable close.

Simultaneous Increasing and Decreasing Stories

Adapted from a Jewish folktale, Phoebe Gilman's *Something from Nothing* gives the reader Joseph's decreasing blanket on the first floor of the house. At the same time, the blanket becomes smaller and smaller, it supplies a mouse family with scraps of worn-out cloth perfect for decorating their house.

Parallel Stories

Frank Asch presents a graphic example of a parallel story structure in *Just Like Daddy*. It's quite easy reading with Little Bear imitating his daddy in most behaviors. In a surprise ending, we see him impacted by his mom in important ways, too. The two narrators tag team in moving us through both of these developments.

Stories within Stories

T. H. Noble's *The Day Jimmy's Boa Ate the Wash* unrolls in reverse chronological order. A girl describes her school's field trip to her increasingly startled mother: crying cows, joy-riding pigs, and a left-behind boa constrictor. The inner story (mom's accelerating reactions) accumulates events while the framing story is told in a linear fashion.

Stories with Linear Time Lines

Every Autumn Comes the Bear targets grades 3 and up. With richly colored paintings, nature illustrator Jim Arnosky vividly portrays a bear's search for a winter den and follows him through the last days before his hibernation.

Stories with Full-Circle Time Lines

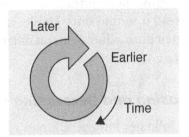

Lisa Wheeler's *Bubble Gum, Bubble Gum* has a full-circle time line. After a menagerie of animals escapes from a bubble gum mess, a bear and a hen get stuck and start the story again. Toad, Shrew, Goose, Bee, and Crow all get stuck on a wad of bubble gum in the middle of the road. Then comes a blue truck, and even adults begin to wonder. Ingenuity and cooperation pay off, but the story has not finished yet, for in this full-circle tale, a bear and a hen start it all over again.

Stories with Rising Action

These stories include the traditional elements of short stories that students will meet the rest of their lives. They start with exposition that sets up the tension in the plot. The action of the story rises and the tension increases until it resolves either naturally or by a decision of one of the characters. Joanna Galdone's *The Tailypo: A Ghost Story* opens with a varmint that sneaks into an old man's house; without hesitating, the man cuts off its tail and makes a snack of it. Later when the varmint returns for its "tailypo," the anxiety rises. This tale makes today's readers quiver much like the first telling of the folktale.

As students recall 5 to 8 key words from one of these stories, they claim that their list of words is writing. In a very real sense, it actually is. A Story Reporting prompt helps them remember what they were thinking when they helped create the list, and they did write the words phonetically on paper. They call out each word in the sequence of the story structure. They explain with pride how each fits into the story and supports the main idea, moral, or lesson. They are empowered to take their list of words anywhere and, unlike Juanita, let the plot structure of the story emerge, engaging listeners with rich and meaningful report.

Exemplars of Story Reporting Entries for and from Emerging Writers

---

Story Reporting of *Fancy Nancy and the Posh Puppy* by Jane O'Connor

Written constructed response to "Tell us about Fancy Nancy's adventure."

FANCY NANCY
POSH PUPY
NABOR
DONT PLAE
SHELLTR

Oral report

Fancy Nancy dressed up. She wore high heels and beads and pretty hairclips. She wanted a fancy dog. The poodle came to her house, but didn't play. Nancy was sad. Her mom took her to the dog shelter.

They found the best dog. They played in the car. Nancy dressed
her new dog up. They really had fun. The End
— Juanita R, kindergarten

Story Reporting of *Watch Your Tongue, Cecily Beasley* Lane Fredrickson and Jon Davis

Written constructed response to "What kind of girl was Cecily Beasley?"

POLIT
PLEZ
TAP DANS
CRTWEL
WOT SAIR

Oral report

Cecily Beasley was not polite. She never said please and thank you.
She dances on the kitchen table. Her mom says, "Get down." Then
she did cartwheels in the mud. She got real dirty. Her T-shirt says
"I won't share." I would not be her friend.
— Timothy B, grade 1

Story Reporting of *A Couple of Boys Have the Best Week Ever* by Marla Frazee

Written constructed response to the prompt "Why was it the best week
ever?"

WAWFULS
BANOKULARS
JAMON
PENGUIN

Oral report

I like Eamon and James. They go to California. It is best week
ever. They have banana waffles. They get binoculars. Their grandma
calls them Jamon. They make penguin costumes and surprise their
grandpa and grandma. It was the best week ever.
— Quantavious F, grade 1

What I Thought You Taught for Independent Writers

The What I Thought You Taught strategy expands the Story Reporting strategy to include all modes of reading/writing in the core genres of informative/explanatory, narrative, and opinion/argument. The strategy is as straightforward as its six-word title suggests. Students can better understand reading texts and instructional lessons by placing them in one of the following modes of writing. They think, "The author was teaching me . . ." or "My teacher was teaching me . . ." in a specific mode of presentation.

Reading/ Writing Genre	Mode of Presentation	Reading Text	Instructional Lesson
Informative/ explanatory	Cause–effect	*Why Mosquitoes Buzz in People's Ears,* Verna Aardema, Scholastic Press, 1975	"Factors That Led to the US Civil War"
	Character sketch	*Abraham Lincoln for Kids,* Jacob Smith; "Athena, Deep Intellect," *The Soul of an Octopus,* Sy Montgomery	"The Lord of the Manor in Feudal England"
	Compare–contrast	*If You Lived Here: Houses of the World,* Giles Laroche, HMH, 2011; *Grant and Lee,* Wayne Vansant, Zenith Press, 2013; *Frog and Fly,* Jeff Mack, Philomel Books, 2012	"Congruence and Similarity in Geometric Figures"
	Description: object	*Empire State Building,* Elizabeth Mann, Mikaya, 2003; *Castle: How It Works* David Macaulay and Sheila Keenan, Roaring Brook, 1977	"Picture Makers and Picture Killers"
	Description: place	"Hogwarts," *Harry Potter* series, Scholastic, 1999; *Imprisoned: The Betrayal of Japanese Americans during World War II,* Martin W. Sandler, Walker Children's Pub, 2013	"Habitat of Nesting Birds"
	Explain a classification	*The Arctic Inuit: Native Americans in Olden Times,* www.nativeamericans. mrdonn.org, 2015	"Characteristics of Mammals"

(Continued)

Reading/Writing Genre	Mode of Presentation	Reading Text	Instructional Lesson
	Explain a process	*How It's Made: Golf Balls,* www.science.discovery.com; *The Nazi Hunters: How a Team of Spies and Survivors Captured the World's Most Notorious Nazi,* Neal Bascomb, Levine, 2013	"Volcano: A Destructive and Constructive Force of Nature"
	Problem–solution	*The Story of Ruby Bridges,* Robert Cole; *Legend of the Bluebonnet,* Tomie de Paola	Children Who Changed History
Narrative	Fiction	*Legend of the Bluebonnet,* Tomie de Paola, Putnam, 1983	"Surprise Endings in Short Stories"
	News report	"What's Causing Texas Earthquakes?" *CNN.com,* May 9, 2015	"Effects of Water Pollution"
	Nonfiction	*Redwoods,* Jason Chin, MacMillan, 2009; *The Family Romanov: Murder, Rebellion, and the Fall of Imperial Russia,* Candace Fleming, Schwartz and Wade, 2014	"Memoirs vs. Autobiographies"
	Summary	*Open Wide: Tooth School Inside,* Laurie Keller, Henry Holt and Co., 2000	"Keys to Writing a Good Summary"
Opinion/argument		*The Case of the Vanishing Little Brown Bats: A Scientific Mystery,* Sandra Markle, Millbrook Press, 2015	"Pros and Cons of City Life"; "Pros and Cons of the US Electoral College"

Independent writers rise to the challenge of telling authors and teachers what they learned from a reading text or instructional lesson. What I Thought You Taught entries allow you to see if what students understand resembles the reading you assigned or lesson you taught. The challenge for students include

- putting new knowledge into their own words,
- using a set number of key terms in a meaningful arrangement,
- explaining sizable amounts of information in few words,
- citing evidence from lessons or reading texts, and
- focusing on writing content over writing conventions.

The guidelines from the "Guide for Writing to Learn" goes like this:

1. Write the prompt at the top of your page.
2. List words you will need to write an accurate and complete entry of what you were taught.
3. As you write a paragraph, explain each word that you use from the list.
4. Let a peer read your entry. He/she will circle the words you have used from the list.

Although the Five Key Practices apply, they do vary slightly.

Key Practice		Description
I	Quantify your expectations for each constructed response.	Quantify the number of key terms and sentences you expect students to use in their response to every What I Thought You Taught you prompt. • For grades 4–8 students, expect 5–6 key words from a word wall or brainstorm list. • Emphasize the need to refer to more than one part of a lesson or text.
2	Write your own personal response to What I Thought You Taught prompts the first couple of times.	Provide your model response to the prompt that you assigned to students. With What I Thought You Taught, it is virtually impossible for students to write an entry that resembles yours, especially when you make your model an original or unexpected one. Make sure you circle the key terms in your model and that your model exceeds your expectations of student.
3	Guide student choices with a simple critical-thinking strategy.	All students read aloud the guidelines in the "Guide for Writing to Learn" for Strategy A. **Note:** What I Thought You Taught entries are always written independently.
4	Prompt specific PALS strategies with each entry.	Using the PALS response strategy you assign, PALs complete the following sentence stem, "The strength of your writing is. . . ." The reading text or lesson determines the genre of the What I Thought You Taught entry.
5	Secure student self-assessment.	Immediately when students finish writing, they complete the self-assessment. 1. "I used key terms with meaning." 2. "I wrote meaningful facts." 3. "I used evidence from parts of the text or lesson." Students then read their entries aloud to an assigned PAL for him/her to confirm (√) or question (?) each assessment.

When you prompt students to construct responses using the What I Thought You Taught strategy,

- Present them with reading texts and lessons in a variety of writing modes and genres (see pp. 24, 162–163).
- Provide 8 to 12 thoroughly studied key terms for them to use fully until you see that they can identify suitable key terms on their own.
- Place them as soon as possible in groups of 3 or 4 to jot list key terms suitable for their writing.

When you provide or lead students in creating a list of key terms, you find

- your model entry provides clear guidance for students,
- student entries provide you with greater details, and
- clearly divulge what students still misunderstand.

By the same token, students

- respond to the prompts more readily,
- show marked growth in the depth of knowledge of their responses over time,
- write explanations that contribute to their classmates' understanding, and
- become confident in providing evidence of the underlying meaning of texts and class lessons.

Since all students are explaining their understanding of the same topic, students' sharing in small groups bring sufficient closure to the writing. Remind students to respond using the designated PALS response strategy as they hear each member of the group present his/her entry aloud.

Exemplars of What I Thought You Taught Entries— Independent Writers

---

Prompt: . . . *about Czar Nicholas II*

Key terms: *citizens, executed, Japanese war, monarchy, Nicholas the Bloody, revolution of 1917, Russia, Russian Orthodox Church, soldiers, Soviet Union, Vladimir Lenin, war, WWI*

Expectations: 4–5 key terms; 5–6 sentences

I thought you taught us that Russian citizens were tired of Czar Nicholas II. He joined wars that killed over three million soldiers and citizens. They decided to overthrown him and his family at the palace. One main person of this event was man named Vladimir

---

Lenin. He renamed Russia the Soviet Union. Soon after other events happed, he started to gain more power. The Czar and his family and their servants were all executed in July 1918. Russians were just tired of being cold, hungry and ravaged by war. The Russian Orthodox Church made the czar and his family saints because they were brave when they died.

— Gabriel E, grade 7

Prompt: . . . *alternative fuels*

Key terms: *ancient decomposed plants, auto fuel, biofuels, bio-mass, bio-products, chemicals, coal, fossils, GVL, limited, natural gas, plastic products, solvent*

Expectations: 4–5 key terms; 5–6 sentences

I thought you taught us about running out of petroleum, natural gas and coal. They all come from deep in the earth from ancient decomposed plants. The earth would take millions of years to create more oil when we run out. So we need to look elsewhere. You mentioned right after plants die, we could use their biomass to make fuel and plastics. These are called biofuels and bio-products. A solvent called GVL will break the stems, stalks and leaves down. Then we can start to solve the problem of limited fuel. I hope this happens in my lifetime.

— Shatina R, grade 10

What I Thought You Taught Prompts and Course Standards

The What I Thought You Taught strategy prompts the greatest variation in student writing among the strategies in *Constructed Responses for Learning*. That is expected since what students think is taught is not a prompt that anticipates a specified response. Some students may revert to an entry of basic recall (DOK 1). Yet the strategy prompts an analysis and synthesis of a class lesson or reading text (DOK 4). Because of this wide range of responses, it is important to place students at DOK 1 and DOK 4 in the same small groups for response. In this way, marginal writers hear and respond to models that show them how to read between the lines of reading texts or class lessons *say* to the richness of what they may *mean*.

The prompts and the exemplars above illustrate ways to use the What I Thought You Taught strategy within a single standard. It is easy to vary the Focused Free Writing prompts drawn on terms from within a standard. Especially important with What I Thought You Taught is prompting them to notice similarities and differences in what you taught by presenting related standards and texts.

For sure, including terms from more than one standard or text is likely to result in extended writing, and well it could. However, short constructed responses are still the safest place for students to practice the art and craft of writing extended thoughts. As you can see, a writing prompt that asks students to explain what they thought the teacher taught by asking them to read *Across Five Aprils* at the same time they were studying the US Civil War.

Prompt: . . . about *Across Five Aprils* paired with Unit 2 of our social studies text

Key terms: *13th Amendment, 54th Massachusetts Regiment, Antietam, Appomattox Court House, Battle of Gettysburg, Battle of Shiloh, blockade, Border State, bounty, cavalry, Clara Barton, Confederate States of America, conscription, Copperhead, Dred Scott, Emancipation Proclamation, Fort Sumter, Fugitive Slave Act, Harriet Beecher Stowe, income tax, ironclad, Jefferson Davis, John Brown, Kansas Nebraska Act, Lincoln/Douglas Debate, minie ball, popular sovereignty, rifle, Robert E. Lee, secede, Siege of Vicksburg, Ulysses S. Grant, Uncle Tom's Cabin, William Tecumseh Sherman*

I thought you taught us about the real civil war in <u>Across Five Aprils</u>. <u>The author</u> showed us the people side. You taught me that the facts were important, too. <u>Bull Run</u> marked the first battle of the war in <u>1861</u>. The <u>Battle of Antietam</u> was the <u>Union</u> victory that helped <u>President Lincoln</u> write the <u>Emancipation Proclamation</u>. What a great day. But the story of Jethro and his family showed us what real life was like. Jethro's three brothers, his cousin and his teacher <u>volunteered</u> for the Union <u>infantry</u> except for Bill. He joined the <u>Confederate Army</u>, and Jethro was almost beat up by men who hated Bill. A man warned Jethro about the men, and maybe saved his life. You taught that war brings the best and worst out of people.

— Joe G, grade 5

Obviously, Joe has the beginnings of an extended writing project. He seems well prepared for it, too. He has a solid beginning. His short constructed response covers what it should, Unit 2 of the textbook and the novel, *Across Five Aprils*. It concludes with a main point—*war brings the best and worst out of people*—that promises to keep the details he knows about Unit 2 and novel on a promising focus.

Benefits Teachers Attribute to the Use of Story Reporting and What I Thought You Taught

Critical-thinking strategies for constructed responses up until now have focused on guided responses. Even the Focused Free Writing strategy (chapter 9) reins student writers into a quite narrow focus. Yet Story Reporting (for emerging writers) and What I Thought You Taught (for independent writers) open the spectrum of responses considerably. Instead of reporting what an author or teacher presented, the strategies invite students to project what the author or teacher meant them to learn—very different indeed. They both guide the task of responding to meaning directly, the students

1. Jot list key terms individually (beginning in grade 3 and above)
2. Explore and create new patterns of thought
3. Practice response structures that help them develop their extended writing repertoire. (argument/opinion, informational/explanatory, or narrative)

They both build on students' tendency to weave their own worldview into what they are learning.

- The Story Reporting strategy

  o instructs emerging writers in presenting a story structure one key word at a time,
  o helps them use their own words in presenting the ideas of an author,
  o provide face-to-face contact with a live and interested audience, and
  o stretches them to present the story line while interpreting the setting and characters.

    ▪ "My first graders' daily writing matured the most as they practiced presenting their thoughts orally to live and interested audience." (Tennessee grade 1 parochial school teacher)
    ▪ "When students explain key words to an audience who can ask questions, they find out what the word *audience* really means." (Georgia grades K-2 academic coach)
    ▪ "I was surprised to see that all our students could adjust their thoughts to their audiences to some degree. They all made guesses on how to word their reports." (South Dakota K-8 principal)
    ▪ "Story reporting showed me that mastering constructed responses to learn was precisely the challenging, but friendly writing initiative we had been seeking for kindergarten students." (Georgia Associate Superintendent of Teaching and Learning)

- The What I Thought You Taught strategy

  o allows independent writers to write freely about what reading texts mean,

- requires them to think about why you taught a lesson, not just what it was about,
- allows them to extract a few key terms from a list of many, and
- teaches them that they can't cover everything you taught in writing on demand.

  - "What I Thought You Taught prompts produces deeper reflections than any other strategy." (North Carolina grade 3–4 social studies teacher)
  - "The three words, *what I thought,* helped our students quit trying to present information word-for-word from class notes or a reading text." (Georgia grade 4–8 science coach)
  - "What I Thought You Taught made it seem natural for students to condense a large idea into a few, well-thought-out sentences." (Georgia grade 6–8 social studies teacher)
  - "What I Thought You Taught challenged my deepest thinkers without intimidating my most hesitant writers." (Ohio grade 9–12 ELA teacher)
  - "If there is a culminating strategy for constructed responses for learning, this is it. My students are ready for longer research and writing." (Georgia grade 6–8 academic)

- What emerging writers say about the Story Reporting strategy:

  - "My words help me remember the story."
  - "We don't have to write the whole story."
  - "People listen and ask questions."

- What students say about the What I Thought You Taught strategy:

  - "We don't have to explain ideas just like the teacher did."
  - "We get to act like we are teaching the lesson."
  - "Like say, how I explain *photosynthesis* is just as important as the author's explanation."
  - "What I Thought You Taught helps me see what I'm thinking about really complicated ideas."
  - "I can write a whole research article in five sentences!"
  - "It's easier to understand a kid's explanation of *velocity* or *amplitude* (physical science) than the one in the book."

Summing Up

More than other pairs of strategies for writing constructed responses, The Story Reporting and What I Thought You Taught strategies develop students' sense of audience. In so doing, both strategies make it natural for students to trust their own version of the ideas in texts and lessons. No more trying to recall the ideas word-for-word as presented. Both strategies spotlight the central role of PALs strategies in the Five Key Practices. In short, both provide the scaffold needed by emerging and independent writers to attend more to the purpose of their writing as they write. They are ready for the next chapter, which introduces argument/opinion responses.

Suggested Readings

More Stories That Help Emerging Writers See What Authors Mean

Decreasing Stories In shopping with Ruby for grandma's birthday gift in Rosemary Well's *Bunny Money*, Max has to satisfy his thirst, then hunger, and finally clean his dirty clothes. It appears certain that the money will run out before they find the gift, but actually, the smaller amount is just the right amount to buy her the perfect gift.

Increasing Stories There are entertainingly silly versions of this structure. In Jules Feiffer's *Bark, George*, a vet discovers that her puppy, George, has swallowed increasingly larger animals until he falls ill. A bit more complex, the increasing rain and growing mushrooms present parallel sequences in Mirra Ginsburg's *Mushroom in the Rain*.

Increasing and Decreasing Stories In Pat Hutchin's *The Doorbell Rang*, children must share a decreasing number of cookies each time a visitor drops into the story. The ending is not forgone; look out for a surprise ending.

Parallel Stories In Shutta Crum's *Click!*, two stories parallel one another. One is about a polar bear cub, and the other about a boy and his first camera. It's interesting that both stories conclude with the mothers of bear and boy coaching them the skill of hunting and the art of photography. In the opening of *Meanwhile Back at the Ranch*, T. H. Noble convinces us that nothing ever happens in Sleepy Gulch. Then Farmer Hicks and his wife, Elna, find themselves on parallel journeys. Noble switches back and forth between the two characters and their situations in a very enjoyable read.

Stories with Full-Circle Time Lines In Bill Martin and John Archambault's *Chicka Chicka Boom Boom*, it's curious that numbers climb up in a tree where they get in trouble. After they fall and recover, it's obvious they want to do it all over again. As the story proceeds full circle, students learn the alphabet. In the first of Laura Numeroff's popular series of circular tales, *If You Give a Mouse a Cookie*, published in Spanish and English, the story begins with a boy giving a mouse a cookie. What a surprising domino effect this triggers.

Stories with Linear Time Lines In *The Very Hungry Caterpillar*, the now-classic story marked by Eric Carle's beautiful collages, a very hungry caterpillar eats and grows. After a caterpillar frees itself from a cocoon, the story line emphasizes each day of the week. Each includes all the food caterpillars eat. In Andrea Zimmerman and David Chemesha's *Trashy Town*, The story follows a day in the life of Mr. Gilly a trash collector. With a refrain at every stage of the timeline, the story emphasizes the times of the day.

Story with a Story Allen Say's *Kamishibai Man* is a story within a story: the tale the elderly storyteller tells reveals why he no longer performs his art (grades 3 and up). Another story within a story, the art of the Kamishibai man (a traveling storyteller) is relived by an elderly storyteller who returns to his old neighborhood to relive his life. It's obvious that this art no longer exists, and reasons are obvious. In David Wiesner's *The Three Pigs*, the three pigs extract themselves from the story line of this familiar tale. They are joined by a rescued dragon and cat as they outsmart the wolf.

Other Resources

Shutta Crum, "Story Skeletons: Teaching Plot Structure with Picture Books," *Book Links*, May 2006 (31–34), www.ala.org/booklinks
www.justbooksreadaloud.com/IndexCategory.php?t=ARLevel&p1=1&p2=

Chapter 11

Prepping for Arguments

Unlike several previous chapters, the strategy for argument/opinion writing among emerging and independent writers is identical, Either . . . Or. The rational is straightforward and almost too obvious to mention. From the time we are born, we humans have and express opinions without prompting. My first daughter did not like pureed beets and let us know before her first birthday. I tried not to take it personally, but my wife and I prided ourselves in making our newborn all of her solid foods from fresh, organic fruits and vegetables. Yet whenever one of us fed her this nutritious treat, Cortney pushed the red slush back out seemingly before she had time to taste it. Since we had so many beet cubes in the freezer, we tried mixing it half and half with applesauce. That only led to wasting applesauce that suffered the same fate as the beets.

As new parents, we finally realized that there was no winning this argument. Our words were, indeed, completely inadequate to match her choice and resolve. We also learned a similar lesson in making her wait until the developmentally appropriate time to let her do certain things. My wife had read that children were ready for sleepovers by the time they started school, and many were not ready even then. Yet our firstborn announced her first sleepover sometime during her second year, calling us from the next-door neighbor's house and asking me to please bring her new pajamas over to Megan's house right away.

All of this is to say that no one needs to burden themselves with choosing the best time to insert opinion pieces or argument essays into the curriculum. Our current curriculum prompts us to make second graders thoroughly aware of the nature of opinion writing. That is a fine gesture, and I know that folks who made that well-researched decision were convinced they made the right choice. Yet just recently in a kindergarten class, I met Tybee who found pictures in magazines that stimulated her message in writing for that day. She showed me a picture of the picture-perfect kitchen. Stainless steel appliances, six-burner gas range, 40" flat-screen TV, multiple ovens with butcher-block counters.

It was typical of half-page spreads in *Southern Homes,* a widely circulated publication of decorating and redecorating upscale homes. She then proceeded to write the opinion that was bubbling inside her and ready to burst forth. She taped the picture at the top of her journal page, then began with the title

In the Kichin

I sighed and stood at a distance knowing she would soon have a description of the picture in writing, all sweetness and light, no doubt. Then I watched with amazement as what seemed to be a response in the informative/explanatory genre, quickly switched to bold opinion.

> Will you mayhave seen a kichin like mine becasue my kichin is way messe. Why is it all ways messe. Will because we always have a lot of food and or kichin. An some times my sister and my dog messes up the kichin. An then she is in big truble. And shes only three years old! An some times my dog has to go to the bathroom and he mesd in the kichin. But it is way big. An we have a large refrigorader. But still it's always messe. The end

How did that happen? Tybee found the picture in a magazine at a learning station, clipped it free with the scissors and announced, "I'm writing about this picture." She had me fooled; I assumed what she was thinking, and I was wrong. The picture of pristine beauty did not spawn such opposing thoughts. It was the other way around. Tybee harbored those thoughts about her *way messe kichin* that she experiences every morning and found the perfect picture to let her write what she was thinking. Let most kindergartners, gluing in the picture was just doing what she was asked to do.

I've heard a number of K-2 trainers claim that it may be harmful to prompt students to craft an opinion before second grade. It is fine to model opinion writing but do not exacerbate the stress of the K-1 learning curve by assigning opinion writing prematurely. Tybee gives the best response to this advice. When students hold strong opinions, it is the right time for them to write their way through them. After all, the way the ELA standards for second grade read is that students need to be able to present their opinions in writing with a certain degree of confidence. If we expect students to write with confidence, they will need to start well before second grade.

This is just one reason for making sure that the Either . . . Or strategy appears when K-12 students first begin school and remain in a prominent place until they are graduating seniors. The human brain is born thinking with opinions like my newborn daughter, Cortney. Every newborn is like she was. In grades K-1, students write the way their minds lead them regardless of the design of the writing task or the wording of the prompt. Tybee earned the right to receive her personal copy of My Writing Journal, a 24-page booklet of lined page with a half-page on every fourth page for her to find a magazine photo that speaks to her and reminds her of something she would like to write about. Her teacher, Mrs. Hauk, prompted the writing in informative/explanatory genre. She was following the tradition that kindergarten students should only be expected to write stories (narrative genre) and describe pictures (informative/explanatory genre). Yet what Tybee showed her and me was that many of the pictures elicited opinion pieces and narrative or informative/explanatory ones. In chapter 7, Timothy showed us the power of the human mind to view the world and every task with strong opinions (p. 94). His teacher modeled a Quad Cluster that explained why *cousin* was the different word from *mother, sister*, and *brother* because the three belong to the nuclear family and *cousin* does not. He began by dutifully following his teacher's lead, only to change his choice to *mother* in his second sentence. His mind saw the differing feature in the cluster was "generation," not "nuclear family" as presented in the teacher's lesson and her written model.

There are other reasons for starting students writing in the argument/opinion genre early and emphasizing it up until they move onto their choice of colleges or are career bound. The prevalence and importance of argument/opinion writing fills a number of entire books on composition and rhetoric. This chapter will have to suffice to give the power of argument writing its due. All of this is to recommend that you recognize all students come to you as well-practiced argument/opinion thinkers. They are even practiced at making their claims in writing. What they need our help with is supporting their claims convincingly and recognizing that there are always alternative claims that deserve their consideration. Your students do not have to become confident debaters during their time with you, but their written artifacts that make claims, support them convincingly, and recognize and address alternate claims need to grow in measurable ways. That seems like a daunting task, but in the simplicity and clarity of the Either . . . Or strategy, you have an instructional tool that is up to the challenge.

Either . . . Or Responses with Emerging Writers

The procedure for creating language experience chart stories fits the minds of emerging writers. You have seen that it helps them write stories and explain procedures. It is no wonder that teacher-modeled writing on a flip chart is the best way to introduce writing an opinion piece as well. I introduced the opinion genre to a group of kindergartners late in the school year, just prior to mother's day, and thus the topic. As we discussed how we may choose to go about writing, I heard the phrase "Don't forget" several times, so I placed this title on the chart:

Don't forget Mother's Day

I saw the title capture their imaginations, and the sentences came rolling out.

Never forget it. (Juan)
There are pretty cards. (Kweong)
We always go out for dinner. (Tybee)
It will make mama cry. (Billy)
It will make her feel bad. (Cara)
Daddy will get in trouble. (Melvin)

As follow-up, Tybee wrote her own version of the dictated story

We nevr forget mother's day. Why? Because it will make our mama sad.
An we always have fun. An we go to Ryan's for diner. We get all the
ice cream we want. An some times mama opens cards and gifts. An we
get to see her new julry. An it makes mama smile. An she says it's the
best day evr. We don't want to miss all this. The end

The others are satisfied with recalling and saying the six sentences on the chart.

Later, the Either ... Or prompt can appear in the sequence of writing prompts on the Log of Entries. Ask those students who can to read the guidelines from the "Guide for Writing to Learn." Emerging writers who are beginning to write on their own find them helpful:

1. Copy the question your teacher provides.
2. Answer it with the first answer than comes to mind.
3. Write 4 more sentences in a paragraph explaining your answer.

At first, the prompts focus on issues that relate to the students personal or school lives. Christopher, grade 1, responds to 2 out of 18 entries in October.

Which is more embarsing having torn pants or the wrong aswer?
    I think haveing torn pants is the most embrassing. Torn pants is the
most embrassing becaues it show your underwear. They coul push you
down a spread the hole. They could stare at you. They coul tell everyboy
you have a hole in your pants. A wrog answer is not to bad.
Which is stonger, an angry bear or bad breath?
    pe you
    you have
    bad breath
    I think bad breth is stronger. Bad breath make me thro up. Bad breath
will scar the bear away. Bad breath will make me have a asthma attack.
The peple will thro up. When you have bad breath, go brush your teeth good.
The your breath will smell better. Or you mite be sick and nede a doktor.

The Either . . . Or strategy helps emerging writers in several ways. It

- Shows them that opinions are natural for them to write about
- Validates their opinions without judging them
- Does not require that their writing be convincing or crafted according to the principals of argument writing
- Helps them see that all opinions have two equally possible points of view
- Helps them listen to and respond to opposing opinions with respect.

Either . . . Or for Independent Writers

Either . . . Or expands with students as they grow and develop. Like emerging writers, the minds of independent writers are awash with opinions.

This skirt is too tight.
Little brothers aren't really necessary!
I am old enough to stay up later.

Then, once they become immersed in the curriculum.

There were not any settlers in America who treated the natives right.
Circle graphs are the best way to present data.
We need to protect plants much better or we might die.
Healthy food doesn't taste that good.
Telescopes are the most valuable tool for scientists.

It does not matter whether these opinions can be readily and logically supported. What matters is that students have them and feel strongly about them. It serves students well for them to jot down their opinions and try to defend them in writing as a first step in nurture their skills in crafting an argument.

Independent writers view the challenge of preparing themselves for an argument/opinion quite positively. And with the Five Key Practices adjusted for persuasive writing, they engage almost immediately. Notice that the guidelines for constructed Either . . . Or responses with independent writers is markedly different with emerging writers. Ask your students to read the guidelines from the "Guide for Writing to Learn" aloud with you in unison. Let them complete what each guide states as you move say each one.

1. Copy the question provided; it can be answered two ways.
2. Answer the question one way or another in a complete sentence.
3. Continue writing in support of your answer for at least six more sentences.

For emerging writers, arguments/opinion pieces are accepted as they appear and may serve as a point of discussion. By contrast, for independent writers, the arguments/opinions need to become convincing.

Key Practice		Description
I	Quantify your expectations for each constructed response.	For prompts that you present to students, make sure you quantify the number of key terms for each way the question in the prompt can be answered. This results in twice the number of key terms for students to choose from. Since you are not prompting an argument/opinion essay, it's critical that you quantify the number of sentences that can be written within 10 minutes. • For grade 4–8 students, expect 5–6 key words from a word wall or brainstorm list. • Emphasize the need to refer to both sides of the question and at least one part of a lesson or text.
2	Write your own personal response to Either . . . Or prompts the first couple of times.	Provide your model response to the prompt that you assigned to students. Predict which way fewer students will choose and defend that point of view. Even if students follow your choice when it is not their first one, they are practicing a response that follows the "Guide for Writing to Learn" (see eResources).
3	Guide student choices with a simple critical-thinking strategy.	All students read aloud the guidelines in the "Guide for Writing to Learn" for Strategy C. No group writing on Either . . . Or.
4	Prompt specific PALS strategies with each entry.	Using only the strategy you assign, PALs complete the following sentence stem, "The strength of your writing is 1) opinion, 2) reasons, or 3) details 1) claim, 2) reasons, or 3) alternate claim 1) logic, 2) data, or 3) emotional appeal
5	Secure student self-assessment.	Immediately when students finish writing, they complete the self-assessment. 1. "I used key terms with meaning." 2. "I wrote meaningful facts." 3. "I used evidence from parts of the text or lesson." Students then read their entries aloud to an assigned PAL for him/her to confirm (√) or question (?) each assessment.

When students meet an Either . . . Or prompt, be sure they have copies of the reading text and/or notes or text from the lesson and key words for which they have completed a word study.

With this preparation, students

- deliver their claims and reasons and address alternate claims with greater confidence,
- consistently respond with evidence of DOKs 3 and 4 in their writing,

- contribute to the class' thorough deliberations of the issue, and
- develop an appreciation for both sides of the issue.

Exemplars of Either . . . Or Entries for Independent Writers

The Either . . . Or strategy provides special strength for moving students' progress in learning forward. It sets a way for students to become personally engaged in their own learning at a quite visceral level. Combined with the Five Key Practices, the impact for good is impossible to overlook. There are two examples that helped me see this point.

A veteran, fifth grade math teacher implemented the routine of *Constructed Responses for Learning*, meeting the minimum pacing of 3 entries a week for writing. For the first time in her career, all of students met or exceeded the target expectations on the state competency test for math, including all special needs students. I pored over all of the writing journals for one of her classes and compared the constructed responses in their journals to the students' performance on the state competency test in mathematics.

Takesha's writing caught my attention, and on further study, I saw that the first 17 entries tracked her obvious progress from a glib, superficial thinker to a serious learner in 6 short weeks. With permission, I reproduced those pages and have shared them in teacher training workshops for several years. The experience of analyzing and assessing Takesha's progress became a standard task for training teachers to look at journal writing holistically instead of reading every word and making comments on sticky notes.

An observation of one of teachers helped identify the turning point in this progression. Did you notice that something happens in entry 7? Before it, most of her entries include glowing comments written directly to her teacher:

Dividing is hard if I don't stay focuses and ask Mrs. Banks for help. She's a big help. (entry 1)

Mrs. Banks, thanks for being a great teachers! (entry 3)

All you need is a great and wonderful teacher like Mrs. Banks. (entry 4)

All shout outs to Mrs. Banks for helping me understand shapes this year! (entry 6)

Takesha used each of these sentences to make the sentence count in her entries exceed the expectations and give her self-assessment a plus (+).

Then I saw it. Entry 7, a response to "Which is more important to creating artificial objects, circles or triangles?" Takesha loses the asides, and the entry betrays the deeper thoughts of a serious math student. The prompt set up an Either . . . Or choice, a strategy she had met in her ELA class, and her engagement in her writing was pronounced. She was no longer regurgitating information, scattering key terms with little thought, and padding her entries with filler of tributes to her teacher. She was Takisha, the mathematician. Notice how the key terms strengthen and clarify her observations. These key terms in math may not help her explain a mathematics problem. Instead, they help strengthen the force of her opinion. It shows up in the content and the variety of sentence patterns in her written expression.

> Circles are way more important in creating artificial objects than triangles. Circles make objects move. I see the circumference of circles on car tires. Planes, trains, bikes, strollers and suitcases all move on circles that are similar with different diameters and areas. I can use the formula πr^2 to see how different. Circles make things stand out like stop-and-go lights and fashion designs like polka dots on women's dresses and blouses and slacks and men's ties. Some circles make the foundation for common objects, things like drinking glasses, plates and bottles all have circles as a base. I can probably think of more for circles, but I haven't thought of one way triangles help create objects.
>
> — Takesha W, grade 5

The entry earned a plus (+) for exceeding teacher expectations honestly. Although Takesha was never considered a strong math student, the Five Key Practices helped her internalize math concepts like never before. In grade 4, she missed the target on the state math assessment, but in grade 5, she exceeded it. Mrs. Banks mentioned that she liked to use the key terms and award herself (+)s for exceeding teacher expectations.

A second example comes from a sixth grade social studies class. The teacher, who claimed to be untrained in teaching writing, understood a great deal about the fit of argument writing in teaching and learning. In the study of the geography of the Americas, Ms. Stoneburner knew just the topics on which to base the Either . . . Or prompt. She lived in a school district with consistently high voter turnout and an engaged, outspoken electorate.

Which Is a Preferred Form of Democracy, a Parliamentary of Presidential One?

Key terms—*congressperson, eight years, four-year term, head of state, House of Commons, House of Lords, indirectly elect, less total votes, members of parliament, president, people directly vote, prime ministers, power as citizens, reelections, representative, representative vote for the prime minister, Senate, senators, vote for president*

> I think we have better government in a presidential democracy. We are promised a four-year term before re-elections. I also like it that we

can only have <u>eight years</u> of one person. More people get to be president. Unlike parliamentary. I think that it is better that we vote for him. The author or our textbooks writes that Canadian <u>prime ministers</u> just have to please people in the <u>House of Commons</u> to vote for him. That gives us more <u>power as citizens</u> than they do. We get to elect more than they do. We elect <u>congressmen, senators</u> and <u>president</u>. Canadians just vote for their representative to the House of Commons.

— Kyle H, grade 6

I think that presidential democracy is better. I think this because in a presidential democracy the <u>people directly vote</u> for <u>head of state</u>. In a parliamentary, the people <u>indirectly elect</u> a head of state, I find directly to be a better way, rather than indirectly. I may think this just because I live in a presidential democracy. But I do think it is logical to elect the head of state directly. <u>Canadians vote for a representative</u> to the <u>House of Commons</u>. The <u>representative vote for the prime minister</u>. The parliamentary system is a good system. It has worked well and has some advantages, like <u>less total votes</u> and thus less confusion. Now some may disagree and say that parliamentary is better. These people, in my eyes, are quite obviously, WRONG!

— Lyla P, grade 6

I think presidential democracy should be a better government, because everyone will be able to <u>vote for President</u>. And have a saying in what the president is going to do. Why I think presidential democracy should also be a better government because if <u>everyone has a say</u> then everyone can change how we all live are life. Presidential democracy is better because everyone can get together and vote. Instead of just the <u>prime minister</u> or <u>House of Commons</u>. A preisdental democrachy is better because not only one person in charge of everyone. Also why a presidential democrachy is better because everyone gets to be a part of it instead of a few people. That is why I picked presidential democrachy.

— Ashad S, grade 6

These three entries show that the writers agree, but Kyle and Lyla show that they understand that Canadians do vote. They just vote for the people who, in turn, elect the next Prime Minister. Ashad may understand this fact, but he does not explain that he does with any clarity. Also, notice the power of quantifying expectations. Here, and in most other constructed responses to the same writing prompt, the number of key terms used with meaning separate the student performance the Depth of Knowledge evident in the writing.

- Kyle's DOK 4 response receives a plus (+) for exceeding his teacher's expectations of 5 to 6 key terms with 9 key terms, a direct reference to the "author of the text," and two parts of the text (parliamentary and presidential).
- Lyla's DOK 3–4 response receives a target (◉) for meeting expectations with 6 key terms and two parts of the text (parliamentary and presidential).
- Ashad's response approaches DOK 3 and receives a rectangle (▭) for approaching expectations with 4 key terms and two parts of the text (parliamentary and presidential).

In Ms. Stoneburner's words, the Five Key Practices, and especially Either . . . Or, brought Kyle out of his shell of silence in class. His writing started to display his attraction to trivia, and his growth in defending his point of view about social studies standards was obvious. By contrast, Ashad's grades in Ms. Stoneburner's class were the highest of these three. Yet his writing shows that while he excelled at studying for tests, he didn't take the art and craft of writing as seriously. His entry above is a typical example of writing that is dashed off and left to fend for itself. Fortunately, Ms. Stoneburner was able to help Ashad see this in his writing and he showed improved engagement in writing by the year's end.

It remains amazing that the number of key terms used with meaning can be such a reliable predictor of the quality and maturity of students' written performance. There is no better way to introduce and fine-tune persuasive techniques in argument/opinion pieces than the Either . . . Or strategy. Teaching these techniques one extended essay at a time allows teachers to provide students with 2 to 3 three runs at writing a convincing argument in the entire year. Students eagerly respond to 2 to 3 Either . . . Or prompts every month, show no signs of fatigue with stating and supporting claims, and present writing that over time marks significant progress in the way they think and learn.

Either . . . Or Prompts and Course Standards

In terms of the levels of Depth of Knowledge, the Either . . . Or strategy promotes student writing that stays remarkably similar from student to student, moving back and forth between DOKs 3 and 4. Taking a stand on an issue related to a core standard requires strategic thought. When the writing is dotted with evidence sources related to the writer's claim, it can shift into extended thought. More than any of the other strategies in *Constructed Responses for Learning*, Either . . . Or stands as the transitional bridge for students to cross in constructed extended responses. For extended responses, students consult additional texts, continuing investigation to extend a claim and its logical support.

While it is seems so reasonable to create Either . . . Or prompts within a core standard, pairing related standards fits the strategy even better and helps prompt students' early forays into extended thinking. For example, it does seem quite natural to prompt students to develop a claim and support it within one standard:

Which is the more critical benefactor of photosynthesis, the plant or animal kingdom?

Yet look at the increased depth of knowledge required when a prompt about photosynthesis is paired with a social studies standard.

Which is the more important to life in these United States, the delicate balance oxygen and carbon dioxide related to photosynthesis or the delicate diplomacy between the US and China?

While the constructed response to both of these prompts can be answered briefly in a 10-minute writing session, the second one begs for further inquiry and extended writing essay or report with multiple sources. After all, it raises questions on the minds of all national leaders around the globe. Is making sure that the development of our economic and social progress lives in harmony with nature or our political more important? That question is answered each way by different leaders, and the consequences are quite clear.

Extension of the Either . . . Or Strategy

More than any other critical-thinking strategy, Either . . . Or lends itself to follow-up ELA tasks of reading, writing, speaking, and listening.

- Admittedly, for students on their own, an engaging Either . . . Or response leads to further investigation that leads to further writing, often extended writing beyond the scope of *Constructed Responses for Learning*.
- A mind-broadening, follow-up task prompts students to respond to the same Either . . . Or strategy on a successive day. This time, however, all students respond to the prompt using the other point of view. What better way to ensure a level of critical thought for success in college and career than the confidence in articulating the logic, data, or emotional appeal that supports each side of an argument.
- An ultimate extension of Either . . . Or responses lies in a debate. Students who supported the claim for each side huddle to jot list the variety of reasons, logic, and emotional appeal from their group. They then select 1 or 2 from their group to stand up and follow the debate procedure in defending their point of view against the opposing one.

o As the debate commences, each debater listens carefully and prepares a strong, but civil, rebuttal that follows logically from the point just made by his/her opponent.

o The teacher lists on a projected screen, the points made by each side as a way to assess the performance of each side at the debate's conclusion.

Benefits Teachers Attribute to the Use of the Either . . . Or Strategy

The Either . . . Or strategy

1. offers a surefire prompt for engaging students in their learning at a personal level;
2. requires students to double the number of terms from which students can select the key terms that best support their point of view;
3. requires students to take one side or the other on an issue, not both;
4. engages students at a visceral level to the point of further investigation; and
5. ensures that students see and appreciate both sides of an issue. Their opponents are friends and classmates who are disagreeing with them, and they "see what they mean."

All of the previous strategies focus primarily on the presentation of information outside of the student writer. Either . . . Or makes it impossible for students not to become involved at a very personal level.

- Either . . . Or for emerging writers

  o allows opinion pieces to appear in student writing naturally,
  o helps them see that every opinion benefits from several reasons,
  o points out that the teacher's model writing is for more than imitation,
  o makes them aware that there is more than one way to understand an issue, and
  o teaches them that opinion writing does not follow a formula. It follows the facts and logic and adds the writer's emotional energy. Without direct instruction, persuasive techniques begin appearing in students' responses naturally.

    ▪ "I was always taught that informational and narrative writing were developmentally appropriate for K-1. The Either . . . Or strategy has opened my eyes to my K-1 students' readiness for writing short opinion pieces." (South Dakota grade 1 parochial school teacher)
    ▪ "Our students love the Quad Cluster and Acrostic, but their writing really begins to show growth in their responses to Either . . . Or prompts." (Georgia grades K-2 academic coach)

- "With all of the other strategies, my students focus on counting key words and sentences. It's with Either . . . Or that they focus less on those and more on what they think." (South Carolina kindergarten public school teacher)
- "When I introduced the Either . . . Or strategy, most students declared *I'm not finished* when I called time. (North Carolina lower elementary school Montessori teacher)

- Either . . . Or for independent writers

  o shows them that printed information is not be taken without question,
  o helps them see that alternate claims may be a viable as their claims,
  o helps them begin the work of examining their own claims objectively,
  o demonstrates that stating a claim clearly is only the beginning of a significant, written argument,
  o lets them see that disagreements can, and ought to be, discussed civilly and respectfully,
  o helps them see that convincing writing is often straightforward and to the point, and
  o makes it obvious that writing with a light touch improves the effectiveness of an argument.

    - "As we worked through each of the critical-thinking strategies, Acrostic, then Quad Cluster, the Copy and Continue became my favorite. Either . . . Or is the favorite for most of my students." (Georgia middle school social studies teacher)
    - "For the first time, *I'm* writing arguments I'm proud of, and it motivates my students to engage in the issues of environment science." (Georgia high school science teacher)
    - "All these critical-thinking strategies make great formative assessment. The entries show me what the students understand. But the Either . . . Or entries are the ones that show me their growth as writers." (Georgia high-school ELA teacher)
    - "I thought about what was different about Either . . . Or for a long time. Most strategies help students understand what is in a text and what the author means. In Either . . . Or they begin to understand what they think as readers of arguments." (South Dakota grade 7–10 ELA teacher)
    - "I had to have patience with Either . . . Or responses. First they had less substance than responses to other strategies. So I increased the number of key terms with mean that I expected. The substance started to appear." (Georgia grade 9–10 social studies teacher)

- What emerging writers say about the Either . . . Or strategy:

  o "I get to write what I think."
  o "Little kids have opinions, too."
  o "Either . . . Or helps me write the longest stories ever!"
  o "Sometime I don't want to write another story,"
  o "Reasons are cool. I like to think of them."

- What students say about the Either . . . Or strategy:

  o "I think I'll be an opinion writer when I grow up."
  o "It gets tiring to write about lessons and texts. I helps me more to write what I think."
  o "Either . . . Or helps me understand constructed responses better."
  o "The debates after we write an Either . . . Or entry teaches me a lot."
  o "I never thought there were different ways of looking at history. Now I know that the opinion of the writer matters a lot to the presentation of historical fact."
  o "I wish I could always write my opinion, but I know I need to get better at explaining other peoples' opinions."
  o "If you really want to know what I've learned about history, give me an Either . . . Or."
  o "I think up Either . . . Or prompts when I'm at home or on the playground. Like which is better exercise, the monkey bars or the climbing wall? I could answer that one both ways."

Summing Up

It actually takes more than a chapter to sum up the power of responding to Either . . . Or prompts, but there are key points to remember. The strategy is absolutely appropriate for all student writers, K-12. It is the preferred strategy of many students, yet it needs to remain just one part of an instructional routine that includes a variety of critical-thinking strategies. It is a strategy that helps many students become engaged in learning at a more personal level. It may be a strategy that accounts for a significant percent of students' growth in thinking about new knowledge. Last, it is a critical-thinking strategy that promotes a greater variety of sentence patterns and language maturity.

Section III
An Ultimate Learning Routine

Chapter 12

Putting It All Together

In the first eleven chapters, you experienced the elements of *Constructed Responses for Learning* that lead to peak-performance learning of your students in every class. Chapter 2 introduced the Five Key Practices that remind you of your critical role in setting the practices in motion.

1. You quantify teacher expectations, including the
   - number of key terms students use with meaning,
   - number of meaningful sentences they produce, and
   - parts of a text or lesson from which they cite evidence.
2. You model teacher writing by
   - writing a model constructed response to share with your students before your students write and,
   - more importantly, writing along with them.

The practices remind your students that writing is much more than putting their first thoughts in words on the page:

1. They follow the guidelines of the critical-thinking strategies (free download at www.routledge.com/9781138931046). Once students master a variety of strategies, you and they discover which provide the greatest engagement in and understanding of a lesson or text.
2. They respond to each other's self-assessment of their writing with specific PALS response strategies (pp. 24, 162–163). When students know what features of writing they must share with a PAL for a response, they write with greater intention.
3. They self-assess their writing automatically as they finish it (pp. 23–25). Students admit that they
   - used more, fewer, or the exact number of key terms expected with meaning;

161

- produced more, fewer, or the exact number of meaningful sentences expected; and
- cited evidence from one, two, or three parts of a lesson or text.

Additionally, they read their constructed responses aloud to their PALs verbatim and show their PALs the evidence in their writing for each of their three assessments. PALs then respond with

- A check (√ or ?) to show they understand (√) or question (?) the writer's three self-assessments.
- A statement that identifies the strength of the writing. For example, you supply PALs with 1 to 3 PALS strategies like the following to provide substance to their response and assistance to the writer.

No.	Three-Prong Response			Genre
1	voice	pictures	flow	All
TEXT CONNECTION—The writer's text connects to				
2	self	another text	the world	All
EXPLANATION OF KEY TERMS				
3	exceeds	meets	approaches	All
NUMBER OF KEY TERMS				
4	too few	too many	just right	All
CITING EVIDENCE FROM A TEXT				
5	inference	specific details	purpose	A/O, I/E
CITING EVIDENCE ACROSS TEXTS—THEY _____ EACH OTHER				
6	support	challenge	influence	A/O, I/E
PRESENTING EVIDENCE FROM A TEXT				
7	paraphrase	quotation	summary	A/O, I/E
CITING EVIDENCE FROM _____ OF A TEXT				
8	3+ parts	2 parts	1 part	A/O, I/E
ARGUMENT/OPINION GENRE				
9	opinion	reasons	details	A/O, I/E
10	claim	alternate claim	reasons	A/O, I/E
11	logic	completeness	both	A/O, I/E
12	logic	convincing	both	A/O, I/E
13	data	logic	emotion	A/O, I/E
INFORMATIVE/EXPLANATORY GENRE				
14	main idea	related details	both	A/O, I/E
15	main idea	clear examples	vivid details	A/O, I/E

No.	Three-Prong Response			Genre
16	factual	completeness	both	A/O, I/E
17	cause	effect	both	A/O, I/E
18	comparison	contrast	both	A/O, I/E
19	same	different	both	A/O, I/E
20	problem	solution	both	A/O, I/E
NARRATIVE GENRE				
21	beginning	middle	ending	N
22	exposition	rising action	resolution	N
23	character	plot	setting	N

Note: A/O = argument/opinion (A/O) genre; I/E = informational/explanatory (I/E) genre; N = narrative genre

Of equal importance to the Five Key Practices are the 13 critical-thinking strategies presented with student exemplars for emerging and independent writers in chapters 4 through 11. In order to benefit most from the critical-thinking strategies, students

- see a sample constructed response that you have written as you introduce a new strategy,
- read the guidelines for the strategy aloud with their classmates ("Guide for Writing to Learn," see eResources) until they show evidence that they employ the strategy with fidelity,
- practice a new strategy for three or more consecutive times until their constructed responses employ the strategy with fidelity,
- make up entries they miss or return to an entry to improve it and raise their self-assessment, and
- start choosing from among several strategies when constructing responses to lessons or texts.

Also, it is important to remember that any of the critical-thinking strategies in *Constructed Responses for Learning* can be used to elicit student entries at any of the four levels of DOK (p. 15).

For example, you can prompt students with the Either . . . Or strategy to

- Recall and write out in their own words one side of an argument presented explicitly in a text. Their written entry shows that they understand the claim, reasons, and details of one side of an issue (DOK 1).
- Add their own reasoning in support of one side of an argument presented in a text. Their written entries show that they can apply their own reasoning to an argument they have read (DOK 2).
- Analyze a situation that is presented in a text without bias and develop a logical argument that they are convinced best resolves the issue (DOK 3).

- Appraise a situation presented in a text and draw inferences about novel connections they identify in the details. Their written entries show that they have synthesized a new way for creating an argument or identifying an issue and resolving it (DOK 4).

All of this is to say that intentional care in creating and employing the critical-thinking prompts of *Constructed Responses for Learning* pays off in big dividends for teaching (you) and learning (your students at all levels of DOK). All you need is a scope and sequence of writing prompts based on your current curriculum. Since your curriculum is not available to me at this writing, I will call on reading texts to illustrate how simply and easily you can put together all of the features of the instructional routine presented in this book.

Responding to Reading Texts for Emerging Writers

Beginning in the first weeks of kindergarten, emerging writers need to meet models of reading texts that they can respond to readily in their own writing. At first, students follow three important steps until the steps outlast their usefulness:

1. They listen to you read the text aloud to them.
2. They help you identify the key terms that bring the essential meaning of the text back to their minds.
3. They take turns dictating sentences to you for you to record on chart paper as a model for writing a constructed response.

As you repeat this process with small groups of students (5 to 7), one-by-one they will give evidence that they are ready to peel away from the group and start constructing their responses on their own (Step 3).

Once most of your class is participating in Step 3 automatically (even with a bit of impatience), it is time for you to begin weaning your beginning writers away from the group on Steps 1 and 2 as well.

Examples of Reading-Writing Modules for Emerging Writers

In a district of 14 schools, volunteer teachers and all academic coaches met in the district training facility. Their objective was to create writing tasks at DOK Levels 1 through 3 for reading texts correlated to their course standards. They agreed to create all modules so that the reading texts were easy for their colleagues to locate and that the writing tasks prompted writing at all four DOKs. The resulting archive of Reading-Writing Modules created a wave of energy and engagement in the students' daily constructed responses to learn their curriculum standards.

The first sample module was created for grade 1 by an academic coach and first grade teacher.

Reading text: *Frog and Toad Together: The Garden*

Lexile reading level: 330

Students in grade/subject: Grade 1/science

Subject specific vocabulary: *garden, ground, grow, plant, rain, seeds, sun*

Academic vocabulary: *afraid, awaken, chorus, frightened, merry, poems, shouting*

DOK 1 (recall, a summary in the writer's own words)–

Copy and Continue writing prompt:

Toad wants a garden like Frog's. Frog warns Toad that gardens are hard work.

Students read the first two sentences aloud together and continue writing the story in their own words. Then they explain how Toad discovers growing a garden is hard work using 2–3 key terms of their choice.

Teacher model:

Toad wants a garden like Frog's. Frog <u>warns</u> Toad that gardens are <u>hard work</u>. Toad <u>plants</u> his <u>seeds</u> and thinks that they will immediately <u>grow</u>. He plants them and <u>shouts</u> at them to start growing. Of course the plants do not immediately grow. Toad believes that the seeds are <u>afraid</u> to grow. Frog tells him to leave the seeds alone and let the <u>sun</u> and <u>rain</u> fall on them. Instead, Toad begins to think of ways to help the seeds not be afraid and able to grow. He sings, reads stories and <u>poems</u> to help his seeds not be <u>frightened</u>. Toad falls asleep and when he is <u>awakened</u> by Frog, his garden has started to grow (12 key terms).

Student exemplar:

Toad wants a garden like Frog's. Frog <u>warns</u> Toad that gardens are <u>hard work</u> (read aloud). Toad <u>plants</u> the <u>seeds</u>. He shouts! grow plants grow! They don't grow. Frog says com down. Seeds need <u>rain</u> and <u>sunlight</u>. Toad coms down. He reads a poem and falls aslepe. When he wakes up the plants are awredi growing (6 key terms).

— W. Kim

DOK 2 (skill/concept like vocabulary and author's word choice)–

Quad Cluster writing prompt:

garden, plant, afraid*, seeds

Teacher model:

Plants, seeds and garden are alike because they all refer to growing things. Seeds become plants and many plants become a garden. The word afraid does not fit with this group because it is a <u>feeling</u> that the character in the story uses to describe the seed. It is an <u>emotion</u> that you feel, and plants, seeds and gardens do not feel emotion. They just need <u>rain</u> and <u>sunlight</u> to grow (4 key terms).

Student exemplar:

Afraid is different. <u>Plants</u> don't git <s>skeerd</s>. <u>Seeds</u> make plants in a <u>garden</u>. Thats all there is. Afraid isnt in a garden. Its a <u>feeling</u> (5 key terms).

— W. Kim

DOK 2 (skill/concept like vocabulary and author's word choice)–

Analogy writing prompt:

seed : plant :: caterpillar : butterfly

Teacher model:

Seed is to plant as caterpillar is to butterfly. When a seed is planted into the <u>ground</u>, it will transform and <u>grow</u> into a full-sized plant with <u>rain</u>, <u>sunlight</u>, love and care. A caterpillar will make a <u>cocoon</u> around itself, transform, and <u>emerge</u> as a butterfly (6 key terms).

Student exemplar:

Seed is to plant as caterpillar is to butterfly. These are the same. But seeds are a plant. Caterpillars are a <u>animal</u>. A seed <u>grows</u> up to be a plant. A caterpillar grows up to be a butterfly. This was easy (2 key terms).

— Y. Harmony

DOK 3 (skill/concept like vocabulary and author's word choice)–

Either . . . Or writing prompt:

Which is better, to work hard to grow your own garden or to enjoy a garden that someone else grew?

Use one of these first sentences:

It is better to work hard to grow your own garden.

-OR-

It is better to enjoy a garden that someone else grew.

Teacher model:

It is better to work hard to <u>grow</u> your own <u>garden</u>. It takes time and hard work to turn a seed into a <u>plant</u>. Toad thought he needed to sing, read <u>poems</u>, and light candles for his plants to grow, but that was not what Frog meant by hard work. First you will need to plant <u>seeds</u> in the <u>ground</u>. Then with <u>water</u>, <u>sun</u>, and <u>time</u>, the seed will grow. In the story Frog tells Toad, "Leave them alone for a few days. Let the sun shine on them, let the rain fall on them. Soon your seeds will start to grow." At the end of the story, Toad is very excited to say, "my seeds have stopped being <u>afraid</u> to grow." It would make me very proud to see that my hard work would turn into a beautiful garden of plants (10 key terms).

Student exemplar:

It is better to grow your own garden. You can <u>plant</u> water mellen and corn, not brakli and unyuns. Yuck. We learned how in science. First plant the <u>seeds</u> in <u>dirt</u>. Then <u>water</u> it. Frog said leave them alone for a few days. So I let the <u>sun</u> shine a few days. The seeds spowtid and grew big. I get to eat what I want (5 key terms).

—L. Williams

Contributors: C. Carter and R. West, K-5 academic coaches

The second exemplar was contributed by an academic coach and second grade teacher.

Reading text: *"Getting Around Alaska"* (from Readworks.com)

Lexile reading level: 390

Students in grade/subject: Grade 2/social studies

Subject specific vocabulary: *Alaska, cover, dogsled, plow, skis, snowmobile, snowshoes, team*

Academic vocabulary: *fastest, glide, quickly, snowy*

DOK 1 (recall, a summary in the writer's own words)–

Copy and Continue writing prompt:

It is easy to travel from place to place in Alaska.

Students read the first sentences aloud with their class or copy on their paper and continue explaining the different ways to "get around Alaska." They use 2–3 key terms to explain their choices.

Teacher model:

It is easy to get from place to place in <u>Alaska</u> . . . because there are several ways you can travel. During winter, snow and ice may <u>cover</u> the ground. Sometimes, a <u>plow</u> is used to clear off the roads. If no plow comes, you still have several choices. If you have a <u>snowmobile</u>, you can drive right over the snow and go wherever you want. If you have a <u>dogsled</u>, you can hook up your <u>team</u> and go visit a friend. If you want to exercise or just have some fun, put on some <u>skis</u> and go down a hill. If you don't have any of those things, just put on your <u>snowshoes</u> and go for a walk (8 key terms).

Student exemplar:

It is easy to get from place to place in <u>Alaska</u> . . . When the plow comes, cars drive on the road. You can ride a <u>snowmobile</u> right over the snow really fast. Ride a <u>dogsled</u> to. Thats its name cuz dogs pull it. You can put on some <u>skis</u> and ski down a hill. You can put <u>snowshoes</u> on your shoes and walk across the snow. See? Its easy to get around Alaska (5 key terms).

—E. Klopenhauf

DOK 2 (skill/concept like vocabulary and author's word choice)–

Quad Cluster writing prompt:

walk, snow*, glide, drive

Teacher model:

Snow does not belong in this group of words because snow is a type of <u>precipitation</u>. When <u>clouds</u> get full and it's too cold to rain, the rain turns to snow before it falls. Walk, glide, and drive are all ways to get from place to place when snow <u>covers</u> the ground in <u>Alaska</u>. If you have <u>snowshoes</u>, you can walk. If you have <u>skis</u> or a <u>dogsled</u> and <u>team</u>, you can glide across the snow. If you have a <u>snowmobile</u>, you can drive (9 key terms).

Student exemplar:

Snow is different. Its like soft ice. It snows a lot in <u>Alaska</u>. You can walk, glide, and drive around in the snow. You can walk in <u>snowshoes</u>. You can glide in <u>skis</u>. You can drive a <u>snowmobile</u>. You can't do snow. You just play in it (4 key terms).

—M. Mehta

DOK 2 (skill/concept like vocabulary and author's word choice)–

Analogy writing prompt:

skis: snow :: wheels : road

Teacher model:

Skis are to snow as wheels are to road. (The relationship of these two pairs of words is cause-effect.) Skis are blades that you can wear on your feet to cause you to move across the snow covered ground in <u>Alaska</u>. Wheels are used to push a car across the road. If the road is <u>plowed</u>, then the wheels can be used on any road. Sometimes in Alaska the roads are too <u>covered</u> up to be plowed and people use <u>skis</u> or <u>snowshoes</u> instead (5 key terms).

Student exemplar:

I know the answer but its hard to (re)member. <u>Skis</u> go on snow and wheels go on roads. You wear skis to ride on top of the snow in <u>Alaska</u>. Wheels are on cars and cars ride on the road. After a <u>plow</u> (3 key terms).

— O. Gretke

DOK 3 (skill/concept like vocabulary and author's word choice)–

Either . . . Or writing prompt:

Which is better to use in the Alaska snow, a dogsled or a snowmobile?

Use one of these first sentences:

It is better to use a dogsled in the snow.
-OR-
It is better to use a snowmobile in the snow.

Teacher model:

It is better to use a <u>dogsled</u> to get around in <u>Alaska</u>. When the roads are not <u>plowed</u> because too much snow is <u>covering</u> them, a dogsled is the easiest way to get from place to place. If you have a <u>snowmobile</u> but no gas, you can't travel anywhere. If you have a dogsled, all you have to do is go hook up your dog <u>team</u> and get moving. It's fun to have dogs as pets, but if you have a dogsled, they can be helpers (6 key terms).

Student exemplar:

<u>Snowmobiles</u> get around <u>Alaska</u> better. You don't need a <u>plow</u>. Just drive on top of the snow. Snowmobiles are faster than a <u>dogsled</u>.

Dogs are fun pets. But they are not fast and they poop. Snowmobiles don't (4 key terms).

— A. Van Brocklin

Contributor: M. Wong (K-5 academic coach) and K. Feron (2nd grade teacher)

Responding to Reading Texts for Independent Writers

In grades 3–12 of a second school district of six schools, teachers created Reading-Writing Modules as part of implementing a program of constructed responses for learning. Each teacher contributed two modules to the district archive. The format for creating modules for independent writers was the same as for the modules for emerging writers, but the Lexile reading levels of the texts and expectations for the writing tasks were significantly higher. As you see in the following examples, students were encouraged to use key terms other than those jot listed in small groups. The teachers modeled citations to texts in their own writing and expected the same of their students. By the year's end, students were fluently writing constructed responses for learning at least 2 or 3 times a week in five core subjects. The administrators reported that the incidents of discipline decreased significantly, the average nine-week grades of students reached an all-time high, and the constructed-responses items on a new state test were labeled "easy" by their students. Interestingly, student performance on those same test items supported the students' conclusion.

The first reading-writing module derives from the core science curriculum, grade 5 physical science. The reading text is treated as a part of the science unit on electric circuits, so the subject-specific vocabulary includes terms that do not appear in the reading text. This module illustrates that reading texts should not be treated in isolation, but in the context of the course standard they supplement.

Reading text: *"Lights Out," www.readworks.org/passages/lights-out*

Lexile reading level: 870

Students in grade/subject: Grade 5/science: physical science

Subject specific vocabulary: *electric circuit, resistor, switch, conductor, insulator, battery, open circuit, closed circuit, series circuit, parallel circuit*

Note that at this level, students are encouraged to use and count key terms important in the text, but not on the specific vocabulary list created by the class.

Academic vocabulary: *100+ degrees, carbon monoxide, Center for Disease Control (CDC), detectors, electric appliances, electricity, episode, fainting, heat stroke, hypothermia, path, power outage, spoil, subzero, wind down*

DOK 1 (recall, a summary in the writer's own words)–

Copy and Continue writing prompt:

The CDC stated that there are some things we should and should not do during an extended power outage. Their recommendations are simple and easy to recall . . .

Teacher model:

The <u>CDC</u> stated that there are some things we should and should not do during a extended <u>power outage</u>. Their recommendations are simple and easy to recall. We should use a <u>flashlight</u> to find our way around and not use candles. The flames can cause a fire. Turn off all <u>electrical devices</u>. If it is hot, wear <u>loose clothing</u> and drink <u>plenty of water</u> to keep yourself cool. If the power is out for less than two hours, the food in the fridge is safe to eat. The food in the freezer is safer to eat for 48 hours after the power goes out. If we aren't sure if foods have <u>spoiled</u>, it's best to throw it away (7 key terms).

Student exemplar:

The CDC stated that there are some things we should and should not do during a extended power outage. Their recommendations are simple and easy to recall. We should use a <u>flashlight</u> to get around in the dark. Flames in a candle could start a fire. It is best to turn off all <u>electrical devices</u> to prevent damage even though they are on a <u>series circuit</u>. The CDC reports that outages usually happen when it is <u>extremely cold</u> or <u>extremely hot</u>. If it is hot, keep your <u>body temperature down</u> with <u>loose clothing</u> and <u>plenty of water</u>. If the power comes back on in two hours, the food in the fridge is safe to eat. The food in the freezer is safer for <u>48 hours</u> after the power goes out. These are importance suggestions to memorize (9 key terms).
— A. Dooley

DOK 2 (skill/concept like vocabulary and author's word choice)–

Quad Cluster writing prompt:

simple circuit, conductor*, series circuit, parallel circuit

Teacher model:

Conductor is the different word in this cluster. <u>Copper</u> and <u>aluminum</u> wires are metals that conduct electricity when they are wrapped in an <u>insulator</u> that keeps the <u>electricity</u> in the conductor. Simple circuits, parallel circuits, and series circuits are all ways to arrange electrical wiring. Electricity flows along a <u>single path</u> to one outlet in a simple circuit. It flows from <u>one outlet to the next</u> in a series circuit, and it flows to <u>each outlet directly</u> in a parallel circuit. The conductor allows electricity to flow through the circuit (7 key terms).

Student exemplar:

Conductor is the different word in this cluster. Many metals are conductors and so are water and people. So when conductors have <u>electricity</u> they need <u>insulators</u> to protect people from the electricity. Simple, parallel and series are all names for different ways to <u>send</u> electricity to its <u>destination</u>. In simple circuits electricity flows along a single <u>path</u> to one destination. In a series circuit it flows from one destination to the next. Destinations are like light bulbs, computers, refrigerators and furnaces. In a parallel circuit it flows to each destinations directly. A conductor is part of every circuit (5 key terms).

— W. Carlton

DOK 2 (skill/concept like vocabulary and author's word choice)–

Analogy writing prompt:

summer outage: heat stroke :: winter outage : hypothermia

Teacher model:

Summer outage is to heat stroke as winter outage is to hypothermia. According to the author, the <u>CDC</u> describes this as a cause-to-effect warning. If you are not careful when the <u>electric circuit</u> in your house <u>breaks</u> and the lights go out in the summer, you could <u>develop</u> heat stroke. Your body temperature rises above <u>100 degrees</u> and you could <u>faint</u>. In a winter outage, you could develop hypothermia. Your body temperature drops way too low. Power outages in hot or cold weather can cause serious problems for people as well as their sources for food, water and communication (6 key terms).

Student exemplar:

Summer outage is to heat stroke as winter outage is to hypothermia. The author of the text <u>establishes</u> this as cause-to-effect. Look out for heat stroke if the power outage is in the summer with <u>100+</u> <u>degrees</u>. Look out for hypothermia on a <u>sub-zero day in the winter</u>.

This is because your body temperature rises or lowers and you get sick, maybe even die. Further more, the author implies that if heat stroke or hypothermia don't get you, carbon monoxide or spoiled food could. So don't fool around when the lights go out (5 key terms).

— D. Canelli

DOK 3 (strategic thinking)–

What I Thought You Meant writing prompt:

. . . about an electric power outage

Teacher model:

When I assigned "Lights Out," I meant that an electric power outage was a serious matter. In the passage, the author presents advice from the CDC in the case of a power outage. When the lights go out, it means the electric circuit in your house is broken. That's the electric current that flows along a path using wires in a parallel circuit covered with insulation. If the lights go out completely, it means your house has no electricity. If it's below freezing or over 100 degrees outside, you could be in danger of hypothermia or heat stroke within a few hours (9 key terms).

Student exemplar:

The author of "Lights Out" meant for us to realize how serious a power outage is. It is more than the lights are out. I'd just try turning on some the electric switches. If none of them work, the problem is not with our parallel circuit. The power source for our electric circuit has stopped. The CDC states that outages most often happen in extreme cold or extreme heat, and there is the problem. If we are out of power for more than a day when it is freezing, hypothermia is a real problem and my family needs to bundle up. If it's over 100 degrees, we have to look out for heat stroke. I think the author was saying that electricity is very important to us, and we should not take it for granted (6 key terms).

— T. Basheers, grade 5

DOK 4 (extended thinking)–

Either . . . Or writing prompt:

Which circuit would you prefer to be a parallel or a series circuit?

Use one of these first sentences:
I would prefer to be a parallel circuit.
-OR-

I would prefer to be a series circuit.

Teacher model:

I would prefer to be a parallel circuit because I would be able to offer citizens more consistent <u>electrical power</u>. This is because a parallel circuit has more than one <u>path</u>. If one of the paths goes out, the other path/s will stay active. I love this type of circuit because it is in my house, church, school and other buildings. I wouldn't want to have a series circuit because it has only one path for <u>electricity</u> to follow. If one of the lights go out then the whole <u>electrical circuit</u> shuts down. I would be much less likely to cut off power to <u>appliances</u>, <u>carbon monoxide detectors</u>. This makes me happy (6 key terms).

Student exemplar:

First of all, I would be a <u>closed circuit</u>. I would make sure I was completed and ready to go. Then I would be a parallel circuit. It doesn't make any sense to be a series circuit because the <u>voltage</u> to each <u>outlet</u> cannot be the same. The outlet at the end of the series gets much <u>less power</u> than the first outlet. None of the outlets get the full voltage. Since I am a parallel circuit, I have more than one <u>path</u>. If one path loses electricity, it won't bother the other paths. In my parallel electric circuit, your bathroom light might go out, but <u>appliances</u> like your refrigerator keep working. In "Lights Out," the source for <u>electricity</u> to the whole house failed, not just the lights (7 key terms).

— L. McArnold

Contributor: V. Jones and Y. Seller, grade 5 science

The final reading-writing module provides a sample text and exemplars from teachers and students appropriate for grades 6–12. The number of key terms listed is increased. The teacher models and student exemplars show greater comfort with deeper levels of knowledge. Students bring in prior knowledge from a course in addition to the reading text provided.

Reading text: *Georgia CRCT Coach for Social Studies*, grade 7, Triumph Learning, pp. 36–37.

Lexile reading level: 970

Students in grade/subject: grade 7/social studies; grade 10/World History

Subject specific vocabulary: *command system, competitors, consumers, economic roles, government, marketplace, market system, opportunity cost, producers, resource allocation, risk, scarcity, supply, traditional system*

Note that at this level, students are encouraged to use and count key terms important in the text even if they are not on the specific vocabulary list created by the class.

Academic vocabulary: *decision, demand, determine, dilemma, efficiently, freedom of choice, harvest, influenced, performed, referred, tradition*

DOK 1 (recall, a summary in the writer's own words)–

Copy and Continue writing prompt:

The author of our class textbook states that all economic systems are based on how a society answers three questions: what to produce, how to produce and for whom to produce. Different answers to these questions have led to three types of economic systems.

By hand or with a word processor, students copy the first three sentences and continue, explaining the three basic economic systems in the known world.

Teacher model:

The author of our class textbook states that all <u>economic systems</u> are based on how societies answer three questions: what to produce, how to produce and for whom to produce. Different answers to these questions have led to three types of economic systems. They are <u>traditional</u>, <u>market</u> and <u>command</u> systems. Traditional systems let <u>consumers</u> produce their own products, and what they don't produce they can barter with others to <u>supply</u>. Market systems depend on <u>individual decisions</u> to produce or serve and depend on meeting the <u>demand</u> of people they hope use their service or products. In command systems, the <u>government</u> is the decision maker. It decides what is produced, how it is produced and limits what consumers can buy (9 key terms).

Student exemplar:

Our textbook states that all <u>economic systems</u> are based on how societies answer three questions: what to produce, how to produce and who to produce it for. Different answers to these questions have led to three types of economic systems. The first one is the <u>traditional</u> system. People produce a lot of their own <u>products</u>, and they <u>barter</u> with other people to get other produces they need. The second one is the <u>market</u> system. This <u>government</u> lets people choose what products or <u>services</u> they <u>sell</u> in stores. Other people manufacture what people demand and hope consumers choose their brand. The third one is the command system. The government makes most of the decisions in this system. It builds huge factories and tells the managers how much to produce. This means consumers have to buy what producers make. They can't always get what they want or need. Most countries have a combination of market and command systems (12 key terms).

DOK 2 (skill/concept like vocabulary and author's word choice)–

Quad Cluster writing prompt:

command, traditional, market, consumer*

Teacher model:

In the context of our textbook, consumer is the different word in this cluster. It is an economic term that applies to all <u>economic systems</u> of Southwest Asia. Each of three systems answers the question, "<u>For whom do we produce</u>?" a different way. Command, traditional and market are alike since each names an economic system that answers this question. Market economies say that <u>consumers decide</u> what is produced. Producers assume <u>opportunity costs</u> in an effort to develop what they hope consumers will buy. Traditional systems say that <u>producers decide</u> what they want as consumers and produce it themselves. Command economics say that the <u>government decides</u> what <u>producers</u> produce and what is available for consumers to buy. The author simply states that different societies define consumers differently (7 key terms).

Student exemplar:

According to the author of our textbook, consumer is the different word in this cluster. Consumers live in all <u>economic systems</u> of Southwest Asia, but they live very different lives. Command, traditional and market are the names of the three systems. The <u>government decides</u> what is <u>services</u> and <u>products</u> to produce in a command market. It tries to make the right decisions, but consumers sometimes can't buy what they need when they need it. Market economies say that <u>consumers decide</u> what is produced. <u>Producers</u> take surveys to see what consumers want and <u>advertise</u> why they product is better than some other producer. Traditional systems let <u>producers decide</u> what they are able to produce themselves. The author also stated that no country follows just one of these systems. They usually have a combination of them (8 key terms).

— Q. Holcomb

DOK 2 (skill/concept like vocabulary and author's word choice)–

Analogy writing prompt:

command : government :: market : consumer

Teacher model:

A command economic system is to government as a market economic system is to consumer. The relationship of each pair of words is <u>economic system</u> to <u>decision maker</u> (cause-to-effect). The first word defines the second term. In a command economic system, the government is the main decision maker. It decides what is <u>produced</u>, how <u>workers</u> produce it and what is available for consumers to buy. In a market economic system, the consumer is the main decision maker. Market economies let <u>producers</u> size up their market and produce what consumers want or need (5 key terms).

Student exemplar:

Command economic system is to government as a market economic system is to consumer. In each pair of words, the first term is the <u>economic system</u> and the second term tells who makes the <u>decisions</u> of what to <u>produce</u>. In a command system, the government is makes most of the decisions. It tells <u>producers</u> what to produce and how much. Consumers have to buy what is produced. In a market economic system, the consumer is the main decision maker. They listen to <u>ads</u> on TV and compare the <u>prices</u> before they buy. In a market system, <u>producers</u> study what consumers buy and produce what consumers want or need. The author states no system is purely command or market. They are usually a <u>combination</u> of the two (8 key terms).

— J. Smith

DOK 3 (strategic thinking)–

What I Thought You Meant writing prompt:

. . . *about three economic systems of SW Asia*

Teacher model:

In our textbook, the authors meant to present three <u>economic systems</u> objectively, not explain how one is better than the other two. They also made it clear that not any one country followed one system exclusively. For the sake of explanation obvious differences in countries, they stated that all economic systems are based on how societies answer three questions: what to produce, how to produce and for whom to produce. Different answers to these questions account for three economic systems. They are <u>traditional</u>, <u>market</u> and <u>command</u> systems. Traditional systems let <u>consumers</u> produce their own products, and what they don't produce they can barter with others to <u>supply</u>. Market systems depend on the <u>decisions of individual citizens</u> to produce or serve and depend on meeting the <u>demand</u> of people they hope use their service or products. In command systems, the <u>government</u> is the decision maker. It decides what is produced, how it is produced and limits what consumers can buy (9 key terms).

Student exemplar:

In our textbook, I thought the author was telling me that all <u>economic systems</u> are a combination of three different systems. He stated that no economic system is purely a <u>command</u> system, not even Iran. The Iran government makes most of the <u>decisions</u> about <u>what is produced</u> and <u>how much is produced</u>. This limits what <u>consumers</u> can buy in stores. So I think they may buy products from the Internet which is based on the market system. Or they may grow or make products at home like in the <u>traditional</u> system. This is true for Iraq, too. It is not <u>a pure market system</u>. The government decides how electricity and oil to produce, but it lets business people buy products to put in their stores. Like everywhere else, people will make goods and grow products at home. The author doesn't say which system is better, but Ms. Harmon thinks a command more is much more efficient (8 key terms).

— K. Judson

DOK 4 (extended thinking)—

Either . . . Or writing prompt:

Which is a better economic system, a market economy or a command economy?

Use one of these as your first sentence:
A command economy is better than a market system.
-OR-
A market economy is better than a market system.

Teacher model:

A command economy is a better economic system than a market system, especially in a society that is evolving from a <u>traditional economic system</u>. First of all, a command economy is more efficient that a market economy. The <u>government</u> <u>makes the decisions,</u>

of what makes it into the <u>marketplace</u>, and <u>consumers</u> simply decide if they want what the government decides to produce. By contrast, market economies are messy and complex. Consumers have difficulty deciding what to buy because unregulated advertising makes every product look exactly like what they need. <u>Consumer remorse</u> runs rampant in market economies. <u>Consumer protection</u> is a major issue. Second, market production requires <u>incredible risk</u>, and most who attempt to produce (go into business) fail or give up because the <u>competition</u> is overpowering. This leads to enormous producers that control production of many products. These large corporations virtually finance the direction that the market economy takes (8 key terms).

Student exemplar:

I believe that a market economy is better than a command economy. Ms. Harmon says that a command economy is more <u>efficient</u>, and it's easier to be a <u>consumer</u> to buy with <u>no false advertising</u>. But a market system give <u>producers</u> the <u>opportunity</u> to create what they have learned is really good for the economy. Like my Uncle Elli. He created this computer program for learning in schools, and it helps thousands of students learn better. He could not have done that in a command economy. Command economies are slow to <u>produce</u> what people need, and the people their <u>governments</u> appoints to produce may never get around to it. Here's another point. The market economy is winning out because of new <u>technology</u>. On a PBS documentary about small businesses in Africa, the announcer stated that women in small villages need only one cell phone. They use it to arrange with <u>sellers</u> to buy their crafts that they make at home like rugs and necklaces and stuff that other consumers want. The world is become a market economy because it provides opportunity for people to become producers as well as consumers (9 key terms).

— J. P. Harlequin

Contributor: J. Harmon, grade 7 social studies

Benefits Teachers Attribute to the Reading-Writing Modules

Hands-down, of all of the ideas in *Constructed Responses for Learning*, teachers' creation of their own Reading-Writing Modules receives the highest appreciation from classroom teachers, academic coaches, and building administrators. Admittedly, each group sees the activity from different points of view, but the benefits of teacher-created modules group themselves along these talking points. The four writing tasks based on a reading text tied to a core standard in each module

1. level the playing field for all students with reading passages of the length and complexity that you tailor-make to each class,
2. deliver a seamless way to insert supplemental reading texts into the standards of the curriculum,
3. provide an engaging way for students to practice applying their new knowledge of a core standard to real-life situations,
4. present practical writing prompts at all levels of depth of knowledge for differentiated assignments,
5. provide back-up writing prompts when one prompt misfires with a group or subgroup of students,
6. offer 4 increasingly demanding prompts to use on 4 consecutive days when the topic is particularly abstract or essential for all of your students to master fully,
7. present model teacher entries that guide you in creating model entries yourself, and
8. include student exemplars that show how the rigor in student writing appears naturally in the wake of the Five Key Practices.

Teachers and academic coaches say the following about the Reading-Writing Modules they create.

- The Reading-Writing Modules for emerging writers:
  - "I start whole-group writing in the modules about mid-October and let my kindergartners know group-writes continue all year as long as they need them. Like our curriculum director said, one-by-one my students start to ask if they can peel away from the group and write on their own." (Tennessee grade 1 parochial school teacher)
  - "I'm finally getting control of differentiation. Five of my grade 2 students complete a Copy and Continue entry (DOK 1). Another 5–6 students handle Quad Clusters (DOK 2) fluently. 7–8 of them are catching onto Either . . . Or (DOK 3), and three of them have some success with What I Thought You Meant (DOK 4). I'm ecstatic." (Georgia grade 2 public school)
  - "I see why I've never gotten DOK 3 and 4 writing from my second graders. I didn't expect it or model it." (Georgia grade 2 public school teacher)
  - "It's comforting to know that when one prompt doesn't show the understanding my teachers expected they have three more prompts on the ready with teacher models and student exemplars." (Georgia grades K-5 academic coach)

- The Reading-Writing Modules for independent writers:

  - "I thought that creating Reading-Writing Modules was just something extra. After I created two, I found them to be the easiest way to differentiate instruction in my inclusion classes." (Tennessee grade 8 Special Ed, ELA/social studies teacher)
  - "Since the Reading-Writing Modules, I'm using strategies like Analogy and Either . . . Or much more often. They prompt much more insightful writing from my students." (Georgia grade 9 coordinate algebra teacher)
  - "Students listen to or read the prepared teacher models and students exemplars and get busy writing more rigorous entries." (grade 5 social studies teacher)
  - "My coworkers and I had been freaking out about the demands of new constructed responses for assessment on our state tests. Since our students completed six months of Reading-Writing Modules, they declared the test items *easy, a cinch, piece of cake.*" (Georgia grades 4–8 science coach, Georgia)
  - "It's neat to have a way to prepare students to master constructed responses in testing without sacrificing the full mastery of the course standards." (Alabama grade 8 math teacher)
  - "Before *Constructed Responses for Learning,* no one could convince me that my Title I students could be creating constructed responses at DOK 3 and DOK 4. This has been a remarkable personal discovery for me." (Georgia grade 9–12 Special Education teacher, Georgia)

- What emerging writers say about the Reading-Writing Modules:

  - "I can read [remember the meaning of all of the sentences] all of the chart stories on our wall."
  - "They help me remember everything about the stories."
  - "Ms. Kennedy let me write my own story by myself today!"
  - "I'm good at new kinds of writing."
  - "We get to pick the writing we want."

- What independent writers say about the Reading-Writing Modules:

  - "We are not writing on the same writing prompts as everybody else in the class anymore. Mr. Rodriguez gives us all different prompts."
  - "DOK 3 and DOK 4 topics are easier for me to write about."
  - "My DOK 3 responses are starting to get really long. They are kind of fun."
  - "I was really tired of just writing summaries. DOK 2 and 3 are like games that make me think."
  - "What I Thought You Meant makes me try to figure out what the writer was really up to. I like reading between the lines. Nobody ever told me I was supposed to do that before!"

- "Extra reading texts help us see why we are studying standards in class. The texts make the standards more interesting."
- "Now my favorite strategy is Analogy. I've started making my own. Mr. Stack asked to use one of my Analogy prompts for the next American Literature text. He says thanks for the help."

Summing Up

Indeed, Reading-Writing Modules bring new life to the study of course standards. Yet it is clear that the operative term here is not "new," but rather "life." Reading texts as regular supplements to all course standards makes sound sense. By the testimony of teachers and students alike, reading texts from current sources provide the dimension of real-life application to student learning. Textbooks and course guides have improved enormously over the last few decades, but there is something energizing about reading a current reading selection written by a person other than the teacher or textbook author. As I mentioned in the introduction to this book, I chose supplemental reading texts on my friend and colleague Donald Grave's suggestion that we teachers let assessment inform our instruction. Yet it is in my current experiences with creating Reading-Writing Modules with teachers that I fully appreciate the wisdom of Graves's advice. With the regular inclusion of Reading-Writing Modules for learning, you and I are not stopping to "teach the test." Yet we are doing an admirable job of preparing students for annual tests without sacrificing the core standards set to ensure success in college and career. Thank you, Mr. Graves.

Chapter 13

Launching a Parting Shot

As I looked to complete the final chapter of *Constructed Responses for Learning*, an unusual memory of my high school graduation commencement appeared on my mental radar. It reminded me of how little my classmates and I realized about word derivations. I was invited to address my classmates about the significance of our commencement exercise, accepted it, and began to prepare a talk that was worthy of the final chapter of our high school years. Following my English teachers' repeated directions, I looked up *commencement* in the dictionary and met words that caught me completely off guard. To my surprise, I read words like *beginning, start, opening, outset*, not a word about *ending* at all. A second definition restricted to North America, mentioned commencement exercise at the conclusion of training in preparation for an important new stage of life. I remembered my high school teachers telling us that what they were teaching was relevant to later life. Obviously, the onset of that ambiguous life began with this commencement ceremony. In that talk to my classmates, I ended up saying very little of what I had first thought I would.

That is the way launching this final chapter feels. For over three decades, I have trained K-12 teachers as graduate-level students who receive Professional Learning Units for the training then watched them move back into their schools to implement what they learned. As I followed up on a sample of teachers, I observed some things that the most successful ones had in common.

They Set Up Model Classrooms

This may be a tough one. I know what it is like when teachers find new ideas that show the promise of *Constructed Reponses for Learning;* it's hard to stay quiet about them. Yet that is exactly what one successful teacher after another did. On a follow-up call to an elementary school, I heard the principal say to me with resignation, "I spent a lot of money to send my teachers to your workshop, and I have not heard much out of any of them yet." I smiled inside me, although the comment did give me pause; I did not know quite what to expect on my next onsite training day. When I arrived at the school, it became obvious that the teachers took their training seriously and behind closed doors had indeed erected model classrooms. I entered the first room.

The **Focus Board for Writing** was the first feature that caught my eye as I entered the room full of fifth graders.

The interactive Log of Entries and the "Guide for Writing to Learn" wall charts covered the left end of the display.

A pair of student exemplars that exceeded, met, and approached expectations filled up the center.

The plus-target-bar rubric filled the top right corner with a clear sleeve of PALS response strategies beneath. The visible strategy in the front of the sleeve was *Data-Logic-Emotional Appeal*. I knew immediately that Opinion was the current writing genre.

Crates of student journals labeled Group 1 through 4 were shelved neatly beneath the outside wall of windows.

A table identified as **Visitors' Writing Table** stood against an inside wall and drew me to it. There were actually three student journals in place with directions for visitors to follow:

1. Copy the last entry you see on the Log of Entries wall chart on the first available line of page 8.
2. A student will come and show you a model entry for you to follow as you write along with us.
3. Do the best you can to meet our teacher's expectations of number of sentences and number of key terms.
4. Keep your pencil moving until our teacher signals us all to stop.
5. Trust your thoughts!
6. Enjoy writing what you are thinking!

—Ms. McHenry's class

I experienced the visitors' writing table first hand. A student volunteer showed me where the key words for the day were listed. He also handed me copies of a **Picture Makers** page and **Picture Killers** page, telling me to add 2 to 3 Picture Makers to my writing, cross out the Picture Killers, and replace them with better terms after I finished writing. I did as I was told.

The teacher also had three wall posters on display that displayed **clipart of a voice, a picture,** and **flow** with the signatures of some of the students beneath each. My volunteer helper explained that, after he writes, he reads his writing aloud to his PAL. She states that his voice, pictures, or flow stood out in his writing that day. He then signs his name on the corresponding chart.

The *VOICE* in my writing stood out today.

_____
_____
_____
_____
_____
_____
_____
_____
_____
_____
_____

The *PICTURES* in my writing stood out today.

_____
_____
_____
_____
_____
_____

_____
_____
_____
_____
_____
_____
_____
_____
_____

The *FLOW* in my writing stood out today.

_____
_____
_____
_____
_____
_____
_____
_____
_____
_____
_____
_____
_____
_____
_____
_____

When I complimented the teacher on the six guides for visiting adults that were obviously written from the students' point of view, she deflected my comment with, *They were just echoing what they heard me say all Fall.* If that were the case, both she and they had impressive recall of what they were taught.

They Followed a List of Key Practices and Strategies

The list of Five Key Practices and 6 strategies may seem to be quite lengthy. Yet the point to keep in mind here is that these 11 points secure the desired benefits that all teachers say they want.

- Saved time because student PALs provided immediate, tactful, and substantial feedback to the quality of each other's writing
- Increased time for differentiated instruction
- Expanded mastery of the language of a core subject area
- An efficient system for active learning, one that provides students with

  - Practice by doing
  - Writing prompts that promote all levels of Depth of Knowledge
  - Preparation for open-ended test items without sacrificing mastery of core standards.

Reminders of Key Practices and Strategies

Five Key Practices

_____ (1) Post my **quantified** teacher expectations for each journal entry. Include

    _____ Number of sentences

    _____ Number of key terms (subject-specific and academic vocabulary)

_____ (2) Write **model** journal entries with students.

_____ (3) **Guide** students thought with critical-thinking journal strategies.

_____ (4) Prompt **PALS** response strategies effectively.

_____ (5) Secure a pattern of **student-self assessment** each time students write.

Six Strategies

_____ (1) Help students write informative entries using the "strategy of the month" at least three times.

_____ (2) Reach a pace of writing three times a week in a target subject area (Career, Technical and Agricultural Education [CTAE], ELA, fine arts, science, social studies).

_____ (3) Insert journal writing effectively during a class lesson.

     _____ Lesson activator

     _____ Summary point

     _____ Lesson close

_____ (4) Demonstrate an effective journal routine for an administrator (annual observations).

_____ (5) Connect the journal writing to educational tools (rubrics, graphic organizers, goal charts, et al.).

_____ (6) Tie journal writing to the essential question of the day.

_____ Review total (out of 11)

_____ Month, year

They Integrated Technology into Their Writing Routine

Forward-thinking teachers have always inserted technology into their routines for teaching and learning, and their intuitions to trust technology proved to be well placed. The first data that described the impact of student online writing appeared in the National Assessment of Educational Progress (NAEP). For over the last 20 years, US students in grades 4, 8, and 12 placed a check in a box if they composed most or all of their writing throughout the school year on a word processor. Interestingly, students who checked this box summarily scored 18%–23% higher than their fellow students who left the box empty.

In the 1980s, teachers with frequent access to technology let their students write their entries using IBM's _Write to Read_ for PCs or _Applewriter_ for Apple 2e and Apple 2+. In the 1990s, they discovered writing applications like the _Writer's Network_ (Compass Learning), later appearing as _Odyssey Writer_. By the early 2000s, Pearson's _WriteToLearn_ provided a tool for summary writing of provided reading texts and even claimed to score the writing for students, issuing a detailed report of their score. Such a claim is at variance with the researched conclusions of the Educational Testing Service (ETS) that demonstrate the most reliable system for scoring student writing includes the scores of two raters, one the computer itself and the other an educated reader from a group of trainer raters.

The _e-rater_® automated scoring engine is ETS's proven capability for automated scoring of expository, persuasive and summary essays, currently used in multiple high-stakes programs. The _e-rater_ engine is used in combination with human raters to score the Writing sections of the *TOEFL*® and *GRE*® tests, as psychometric research has demonstrated that this combination is superior to either machine scoring or human scoring on their own.

www.ets.org/research/topics/as_nlp/writing_quality/

To date, the only writing software that can claim to provide students with writing experiences online that explore all levels of Depth of Knowledge is the one connected to the instructional routine described here in *Constructed Responses for Learning*. *Writing to Win* online includes an instructional routine called Understandings that provides writing prompts for all core standards of ELA, math, science, and social studies, grades 1 through 12. Offered on a learner management system (mysatori.com), it includes a teacher portal with

- A seamless process for importing class rosters from your school database.
- Access to 4 to 8 writing prompts for each core standard of ELA, math, science, and social studies that suggests that teachers provide

  o a list of 6 to 12 key terms related to the standard,
  o the quantity of key terms for students to include in their writing,
  o the number of sentences,
  o the choice of student self-assessment statements to form a rubric, and
  o the choice of PALS response strategy.

- Default settings that require students to

  o use a variety of critical-thinking strategies from the earlier chapters of *Constructed Responses for Learning*,
  o complete up to three self-assessment statements,
  o read their writing aloud to assigned PALs,
  o show their PALs evidence in their writing of the three self-assessment scores,
  o complete three PALS response strategies based on the writing, and
  o write a one-sentence summary of their PALs' responses.

- Management tool for differentiating writing prompts among your students.
- Reporting tool for viewing and printing out reports of student progress by strategy or core standard.

Note that all settings are default and can be turned off or on as you bring each of them into your key practices and strategies of *Constructed Responses for Learning*.

They Created a Literacy Team of Colleagues

Call this team a literacy team and welcome all teachers who approach you and ask, "Can you show me what you are up to?" Of course you can. And you can promise the results like the data reported at www.writingtowin.com when they follow the Five Key Practices on pp. 22–27. Consider the ones who do not bat an eye at the list as members of your literacy team. Tell them they need a copy of *Constructed Responses for Learning* and be willing to get together at least once a month to support each other and hold one another accountable. Tell them how long it has taken you to set up your model classroom. Add that you are incredibly patient and willing to coach them as long as they maintain their resolve. Emailing me at info@writingtowin.com can provide the help you need once you provide an accurate description of the progress you and your team have made.

Best wishes to you. After all,
In the writing comes the learning!